U-BET

I am told it was the fourth jump that found me quite separate from my mount. See page 135.

U-BET

A Greenhorn in Old Montana

by
John R. Barrows

Introduction by
Richard B. Roeder

University of Nebraska Press
Lincoln & London

First Bison Book printing: 1990
Most recent printing indicated by the first digit below:
10   9   8   7   6   5   4   3   2   1

Library of Congress Cataloging-in-Publication Data
Barrows, John R. (John Rumsey), b. 1864.
   [Ubet]
   U-bet: a greenhorn in old Montana / by John R. Barrows:
introduction by Richard B. Roeder.
      p. cm.
   Reprint, with new introd. Originally published: Ubet. Caldwell,
Idaho; Caxton Printers, 1934.
   ISBN 0-8032-6094-6
   1. Barrows, John R. (John Rumsey), b. 1864. 2. Cowboys—Mon-
tana—Biography. 3. Frontier and pioneer life—Montana. 4 Mon-
tana—Social life and customs. 5. Montana—Biography. I. Title.
F731.B37A3   1990
978.6'02'092—dc20
89-24970
CIP

Reprinted by arrangement with The Caxton Printers, Ltd.

Originally published as *Ubet*.

DEDICATION

This record of six or seven years of colorful experience on the Montana frontier I dedicate to my favorite wife,

LESLIE FOOTE BARROWS.

Without her there would be nothing to dedicate.

TABLE OF CONTENTS

CONTENTS

LIST OF ILLUSTRATIONS

INTRODUCTION BY RICHARD B. ROEDER

In the mid-1880s Ubet was a cluster of buildings—a stage stable, barn, saloon, icehouse, the Ubet Hotel, and an old store that served as a combination post office, stage, and express office. The settlement was located in central Montana between the Little Belt Mountains to the west and the Big Snowies to the east, about a hundred miles equal distance on the stage line between Billings on the Yellowstone River and Fort Benton at the head of navigation on the Missouri. The town was the creation of John R. Barrows's father, Augustus, or "Nald," as he was known.

Nald Barrows, a lumberman from Chippewa Falls, Wisconsin, was part of a Wisconsin group that had planned to settle as a colony in Montana. Members of the first wave of migrants first took up lands near Martinsdale on the upper reaches of the Musselshell River Valley in Meagher County. When in the early summer of 1879 the group abandoned the colony idea, Nald scouted out a location for his own family about forty miles to the northwest not far from the present town of Judith Gap. He built a claim cabin and the following year began building what would be his stage-hotel stop of Ubet. When Barrows chose this spot for his stage stop at the south end of Montana's beautiful Judith Basin country, he surmised correctly that the area would soon be settling up rapidly, and the stage line would experience increasing traffic.

Why Barrows called his operation the peculiar name of "Ubet" is not clear, although there are several versions of how he came to choose it. One story has it that when strangers asked if they could put up for the night, Nald always said "you bet." Son John later claimed that when his father approached territorial delegate Martin Maginnis for help in securing a post office, Maginnis asked for a name and Barrows's "impromptu" reply was "Ubet." The name "had the advantage of being unique and short," John remembered, and "the disadvantage of being undignified, but it served."[1] In any case, Ubet it was.

In 1880, at age sixteen, John Barrows accompanied a second wave of Chippewa Falls migrants. The group traveled to Bismarck, North Dakota, by train and from there to Fort Benton on the steamer *Key West*. After several months working as a handyman at a trading post near Martinsdale, John signed on in August 1880 as a cowboy for the DHS ranch, then just setting up in central Montana. The DHS, one of the more famous of the ranches during Montana's 1880s cattle boom, was run by pioneer Granville Stuart and was financed by Andrew Jackson Davis and Samuel T. Hauser, two of the territory's early capitalists. John worked for the DHS through five seasons, and in 1885 he left to take charge of his father's herd on the family ranch at Buffalo, about five miles north of Ubet. The extent of John's formal education is not known. We do know that in the fall of 1882 he accompanied a shipment of DHS cattle to Chicago so that he could get a year's schooling in Wisconsin. Because his employment with the DHS was seasonal, he had time for reading; and the materials were at hand. Stuart's log cabin library at DHS headquarters near Fort Maginnis contained several thousand volumes and was open to the local cowboys. Barrows's family subscribed to several magazines and two daily newspapers, which members of the family read and discussed. John later said he had a reputation as an "idler" because he read so much.

After the cowboy youth described in *U-bet*,* Barrows in 1888 went to Helena and read law in the office of one of the city's leading law firms. While studying there, he won election to the first and second state ligislatures as a House member. Following his admission to the Montana Bar in 1891, Barrows practiced in Helena in partnership with Decius Wade, a noted lawyer and former long-tenured Chief Justice of the territorial Supreme Court.

What Barrows called "eye-strain" took him out of the law office and back to the family ranch. In 1897, for

*Editor's note: Although originally spelled as *Ubet*, the book's title has been changed to *U-bet* for this Bison Book edition to clarify pronunciation and meaning.

reasons that are not clear, John moved to San Diego, California, where he went to work for the Claus Spreckels sugar company. In 1901 he married Leslie Foote, seventeen years his junior. Three California-born children followed. In 1916 Barrows retired and took his family back to the Montana ranch where the couple's fourth and last child was born. He continued to suffer from recurring eye problems. By 1918 he was blind. The shock of blindness also convinced him he was dying. Wife Leslie and sister-in-law Frieda Foote, who was visiting at the ranch, persuaded John that under the circumstances he should record and preserve the tales with which he regaled his children. Barrows dictated to Frieda, who laboriously recorded the stories in long hand and later typed them. The therapy may have worked; John was to live another two decades. But the manuscript was laid aside and largely forgotten.

In 1927 John's bad health took the family back to California. It was at this point, partly out of economic necessity but mostly to keep him occupied, that John began writing on a regular basis with Leslie, who, now having learned shorthand, recorded copy and typed his correspondence. In 1927 Barrows published his first story. *Frontier*, the literary magazine of Professor H. G. Merriam's creative writing program at the University of Montana, carried a piece he would later incorporate into *U-bet* about his youthful move from Wisconsin to the Montana frontier. With the help of Grace Stone Coates, an old Martinsdale friend and the assistant editor of *Frontier*, John also began writing short historical pieces for the Montana Newspaper Association, which sold items to newspapers around Montana.

Late in 1930, Merriam, who was Barrows's brother-in-law, wrote Barrows that he had suggested his work to Dodd Mead and Company, which was soliciting names of people who might be able to write western stories. By this time, Barrows had become upset at what he regarded as distortion of the Old West by remembered movies and a growing body of writings about the West. Back in Wisconsin his own boyhood notion of what the Montana frontier would be like had been shaped by dime novels that "were as fallacious as is the cowboy literature of today" (p. 13). For Barrows, the picturesque features of cowboy life had been stressed to the point of "burlesque." So when Merriam suggested that he tackle a book on the western frontier, Barrows took up the task, hoping to dispel distortion with a more accurate picture of a passing frontier. He took out his old autobiographical manuscript and began revising it.

As a new version of his story began to take shape, Barrows and Merriam discussed possible publishers, including John Day, who was publishing Montana writer Frank Bird Linderman, and a Knopf series edited by Bernard DeVoto. Alfred Knopf personally wrote Merriam that he thought Barrows's stuff was very good but would probably have only a regional market. Barrows complained that eastern publishers had rejected his work because they had long since decided what they wanted in the way of western writing and his work "did not meet their demands."[2] Knopf suggested Caxton Press in Caldwell, Idaho. Merriam, who had been a fellow Rhodes Scholar and close friend of Lawrence Gipson, brother of Caxton's owner, opened the negotiations. In May 1932, J. H. Gipson saw the manuscript and called it "mighty good stuff."[3] But there was still a protracted period of dickering over the terms of a contract. Because of the Great Depression, Gipson feared the book might lose money, and he wanted Barrows to assume part of the financial risk of publication.

After numerous delays, Caxton brought out the book in December 1934, with drawings by Butte, Montana, illustrator R. H. Hall. Although *U-bet* appeared too late for the Christmas trade, sales rose steadily, especially in southern California. Shortly after the book's release, the Los Angeles public library gave it radio publicity and placed it at the top of its list of current recommended books. Then the American Library Association put it on its recommended list. The curator of historical works at the Harvard University Library characterized it "as the most significant literature yet appearing from the northwest cattle country."[4] The popularity of *U-bet* enabled Caxton to release a second printing in September 1936.

U-bet got uniformly good reviews. *Booklist* called it "authentic and well written."[5] The book review editor for Merriam's *Frontier and Midland,* as it was now titled, described it as "an exceptional book" with two salient qualities: "a sympathy that shrewdness saves from sentimentality and a quality of humor that insight saves from caricature."[6] Frank Linderman sent Barrows a clipping of the *New York Times* review. The unsigned reviewer described it as "a lively . . . and dramatic" account of the frontier that combined "authentic facts" with "more or less fictionalized autobiography" enriched by "cowboy and frontier yarns." The reviewer concluded that *U-bet* was a "dramatic and colorful" depiction of cowboy life "not yet well known in books."[7]

U-bet is an old man's reminiscences about central Montana in the 1880s, which saw Barrows's passage from teens to young manhood and the transformation of central Montana from Indian-buffalo country to a land of ranches and rich farms. Did the long intervening years cause Barrows to fictionalize, as the *Times* reviewer thought? Grace Stone Coates vouched for the book's historical accuracy. She said it was written "by an educated, law-trained gentleman" and she would "bank on it being literally true."[8]

In an August 18, 1935, letter to David Hilger, a fellow pioneer who at the time was librarian of the Montana Historical Society, Barrows explained that in the published manuscript he had eliminated the Wisconsin incidents and padded the Montana narrative with humorous stories "typical of the time and giving the flavor of that rude society, which as you know, was democratic, undignified, and perhaps irreverent, but sanguine, tolerant, and wholesome." He admitted to Hilger that he was guilty of only two conscious distortions. He had changed the location of the story of the fitful cat, and he had put himself into the story of the cooks and the mountain lion. Any reader, he told Hilger, ought to be able to separate fact from fiction.[9]

U-bet conveys valuable historical information. To begin with, Barrows correctly informs readers that the transformation of the frontier in central Montana was surprisingly fast. When Barrows had arrived in 1880, everyone had lived a primitive existence with no amenities. By 1886, regular freight and stage lines had brought creature comforts and enabled Ubet's residents to maintain an alert intellectual life and to be aware of public affairs in the outside world. More important to Barrows were the non-material sides of frontier life. There was, he wrote, "youth, health, and strength; there was optimism and courage; a spirit of friendliness and comradeship" (p. 106).

Barrows's description of cowboy life is unquestionably accurate. His account of the equipment, the skills, the daily routine and seasonal rhythms of cowboy life—night herding, trailing the cattle, the spring and fall roundups, and the inevitable stampede—provide details of life as it was in Montana's indigenous cattle business. As Barrows indicates, some things were different in the Texas tradition of cowboying. Barrow's yarns are also superb examples of bunkhouse humor. Some are told with a false gentility but always with an economy of words. A storyteller must avoid a reputation for being windy. The unfortunate circumstances of others and the storyteller's own exploits must be balanced by accounts of his own misadventures. It was fatal to become a braggart. The reader who does not at least chuckle aloud at some of the twists Barrows gives his tales is a real honest-to-goodness sobersides.

Not only are Barrows's cowboy materials accurate, but he also presents a positive but not romanticized view of the Indian. He acknowledges the humor and joy of Indian village life. He also informs us that the presence of traders did not immediately victimize the Indians. Traders altered some of the material aspects of the Indians' lives; but as long as the Indians controlled their economy before the slaughter of the buffalo and other game, they adapted the white man's goods to their own way of life and on their own terms.

The one area where Barrows might be faulted is in his account of the central Montana vigilante raids. In one of the more controversial episodes in Montana history, Granville Stuart led raids into the Missouri Breaks against rustlers. This was a bloody affair. Barrows's account refers to thirteen victims. There were probably far more than that, but the true number of victims is not known. Unlike the Virginia City activities of some twenty years earlier, the raids did not meet with uniformly positive public reaction. Barrows did not participate in them, remaining back at the ranch to herd horses, and he records that afterward DHS employees who were part of the action were reluctant to talk about what took place. Barrows, who greatly admired Stuart, justifies the raids as necessary to "restore security and order." In a letter to Linderman at the time of *U-bet's* publication, he referred to the raids as "criminal" and added that he had heard men talk "of atrocities that would make one's blood run cold."[10]

Is the reader in for an informative and entertaining experience? You bet.

Notes

1. Montana News Association release, April 16, 1934, Barrows vertical file, University of Montana Speical Collections; See *U-bet*, p. 135.

2. John Barrows, San Diego, California, August 18, 1935, letter to David Hilger, Helena, Montana; Small Collections 1265, Montana Historical Society.

3. J. H. Gipson, Caldwell, Idaho, May 20, 1933, letter to H. G. Merriam, Missoula, Montana; Merriam Papers, Box 18, Folder 5, University of Montana Special Collections.

4. *Great Falls Tribune,* July 10, 1936, p. 11.

5. *Booklist,* 31 (February 1935): 202.

6. *Frontier and Midland,* 15 (Spring 1935): 237.

7. *New York Times Book Review,* December 30, 1934, p. 10; Frank Bird Linderman, Coos Bay, Montana, January 16, 1935, letter to H. G. Merriam, Missoula, Montana; Merriam Papers, Box 18, Folder 18, University of Montana Special Collections.

8. Grace Stone Coates, White Sulpher Springs, Montana, December 29, 1937, and February 26, 1938, letters to James B. Rankin, New York; James B. Rankin Papers, Box 1, Folder 2, Montana Historical Society.

9. Barrows to Hilger, August 18, 1935.

10. John Barrows, San Diego, California, December 21, 1934, letter to Frank Bird Linderman, Coos Bay, Montana; Merriam Papers, Box 18, Folder 5, University of Montana Special Collections.

CURTAIN CALL

White clouds send shadows racing on the plain
Where once the wagons rolled on rumbling,
Wind-hurried from the canyon drifts the rain,
Heat-lightning stabs the thunder's grumbling;
Sun-washed, the western passes set their snare
Where once the trails to westward blended.
The whisp'ring sage still scents the desert air—
The scene still stands—
But the play is ended.

—JAMES MARSHALL.

I GO WEST

HE postmark on father's letter was "Fort Benton, M. T." The map of Montana Territory in my geography was splattered with forts, but I found Fort Benton without too much trouble after Aunt Lottie had read the letter aloud and handed it over to me for further study.

It was natural that I should have no clear idea of this frontier outpost, for Fort Snelling and its battlemented stone walls was the only fort I had ever seen, but my picture although incorrect was clear and vivid.

Our mental pictures are painted with the pigments at hand. If my conception of the Montana frontier was extravagantly erroneous it was because I had gathered together a most remarkable lot of misinformation. The dime novels of the day were the authorities to which I turned and they were as fallacious as is the cowboy literature of today.

In my imagination I could see father safe within the fortress surrounded by those Indians, which on the map were shown to be just north of the Missouri River, yet he made no mention of Indians. He spoke of distances, weather, and soil. There was nothing in the letter to cause a thrill. It might have been written in Milwaukee for all the romance there was in it.

From my observation and study of parents, which I had been carrying on for fifteen years, I had reached the conclusion that they were, at times, devoid of imagination, incapable of enthusiasms, dull and earth-bound. Father said that he had made an extended trip on horseback in search of a location for a sawmill. I could not understand why anyone should leave the Wisconsin pineries and travel sixteen hundred miles in search of a sawmill site. The western part of Montana on my map was pretty well covered by the legend, "Gold Fields." The Wisconsin party had gone smack through them without noticing them. There was no fire, no enthusiasm about the buffalo, and the only reference to the "Red Devils" was that the Crow Indians were "thievish and sassy."

It seemed to me that Montana offered a splendid opportunity for a boy to become an Indian fighter or a scout, and the scout had the preferential position in my mind because the Indian fighters, in spite of their jocose speech, appeared to be under the shadow of some terrible tragedy in their past and to be animated with sanguinary vengeance. The scout, on the other hand, was employed almost exclusively in saving settlers or leading our military forces out of embarrassing and dangerous predicaments, killing only when necessary.

The Montana venture had left several fragmentary families in our little town, and with them I had traced the progress of the pioneer party during the summer of 1879 across the Rockies to Ogden and to the terminus of the narrow-gauge railroad, reaching northward toward Montana, and thence by wagon for weary miles to the Musselshell Valley.

With mother and the children temporarily housed at the forks of the Musselshell, father had been active in making a survey of the surrounding country. He said that in the Judith Gap, between the Little Belt and Big Snowy Mountains, at a point where the new road to Yogo or to Fort Benton joined the Carroll Trail, he had selected a place for our home, because he thought it a good choice from a business standpoint. He felt sure that within a year or two there would be an extensive movement of settlers into the Judith Basin, as the country was very rich and there had been no serious Indian hostilities for two years. This was somewhat discouraging to a boy who intended to become a scout. There was not one word of massacres or rescues in father's letter, but instead he said that they raised wonderful crops of potatoes, and that oats made a good yield.

I finished the reading of the letter and turned to a study of the map. I determined that if I were allowed to go to Montana the next spring, I would travel from fort to fort and if the Gros Ventres and Mauvais Terres were hostile Indians, they should grow familiar with the report of my rifle. If they were mere geographical areas, I would explore them thoroughly.

Autumn spread her colors on sumach, oak, and maple. Upon a background of white, winter traced a network of naked boles and branches and etched fanciful patterns upon our windowpanes. More fantastic and colorful than the efforts of the season, were my mental pictures of Montana and the frontier to which I was destined. If I abandoned one mistaken idea I built another upon its site.

In accordance with established precedent, winter gave way to spring, and one bright day there was a gathering somewhat larger than usual at our little railway station. A score of stay-at-homes were going to join the adventurers of the year before. Over the west Wisconsin railroad to St. Paul, we made the first stage of our long journey.

CHAPTER II

MY FIRST VIEW OF THE PRAIRIE

A LTHOUGH this was familiar ground to me, I was by no means a blasé traveler. There was nothing to distinguish the members of our party from other passengers, so that at first I had no conviction of the homogeneous character of our group, but when we left the train at St. Paul and proceeded in a somewhat compact body to the Merchant's Hotel where we dined and had our account settled by the leader of our party, it began to dawn upon my youthful mind that we were indeed a band of pilgrims, not pioneers as you would picture them. We were, rather, the non-combatants left in the rear by the real pioneers whom we were to join.

On this brief visit I had my first general glimpse of the thriving town of St. Paul. I was impressed by the number of establishments handling furs and pelts and by the gun stores and shops of frontier outfitters—and here I met my first pawnshop. Imagine a sixteen-year-old boy gazing for the first time into a well-stocked pawnshop window—an

occupation which has never since lost its charm
for me—a window displaying dirks, brass knuckles,
firearms of every description, and all the flotsam and
jetsam of indigence. Under the spell of that window I parted with my entire capital and became
the owner of a bowie knife, manufactured, I am
sure, for adolescence only. This supplemented a
surreptitious revolver of smallest possible caliber,
faulty in every feature of design and workmanship,
which I had obtained after my little single-barreled
shotgun (over my unavailing protests) had been
dismounted and packed in my trunk.

At St. Paul we took the cars on the Northern
Pacific for our slow journey to the end of the rails,
Bismarck. There were no sleeping car accommodations for me and the discomforts may well be
imagined, but memories of the tiresome aspects of
that ride have entirely disappeared. I recall only
the many novel sights and impressions, the exhilara-
tion of my first view of the prairies which was to
be followed by a sense of monotony almost unbear-
able. From the little village of Fargo, on the Red
River of the North, to Bismarck, there was almost
nothing to be seen except the level prairie submit-
ting for the first time to the rude caress of the
plow. Our progress was unbelievably slow and
though I was at the beginning of what I felt was
a great adventure, the bleak uniformity of the

country became oppressive. The sun was bright, the air pure. Strange animals were sighted occasionally, and now and then the carcass or bleaching bones of a buffalo gave promise of herds of live specimens. The young men of our party wasted a great deal of ammunition from the open car platforms, shooting at skulking coyotes, and one band of antelope, entirely beyond gunshot, seemed likely to send us into Montana without enough gunpowder for a salute. The ladies of the party, during our long waits at desolate sidings, searched in vain for spring flowers on the frosty ground.

I was impressed by the immense vacuity of the sky. It seemed present wherever I looked, except downward. "Horizon" had been a mere word to me heretofore, of which I had not known the reality. There was a great deal of talk of the new country to which we were bound. My ideas, formed to some extent by letters and conversation, were still very hazy. We heard that Montana was a prairie country, but the word, "prairie" had no real meaning for me until I saw Dakota. The prairies I had known were open glades in a country generally forested. I tried to picture my future home as an almost perfectly flat steppe. This idea had to be reconciled with my knowledge that Montana was mountainous. It was altogether too serious a problem for a sixteen-year-old boy to solve and was put aside to be considered in connection with later revelations. There was much serious discussion concerning future activities with a comrade of my own age. We now agreed that while placer mining was undoubtedly a lucrative vocation, we should devote ourselves to ranching, but as a matter of course we would pick up whatever nuggets were turned up by the plow. This combination of the mining and farming industries was unique and I regret to say has never been carried out exactly as planned.

It was a long flat prairie and a long journey, monotonous, yet somehow full of surprise and interest, and at last we reached Bismarck.

Bismarck, a straggling frontier village on a bleak, cold prairie, was the capital of the territory of Dakota, the terminus for the time of the westward looking Northern Pacific railroad, the point of embarkation for points on the upper Missouri, as well as a supply point for the gold mines in the Black Hills. I saw much that was characteristically western in this little town. The arrival and departure of the Deadwood stage very nearly satisfied my ideas of that aspect of frontier life. There were a few mendicant Indians loitering about the place, beggars and scavengers all, quite different from the semi-civilized Chippewas of my boyhood.

My First View of the Prairie

A camp for the men of our party was made about a mile and a half from town on the shoulder of a high bluff overlooking the steamboat landing, now the site of one of the abutments of the Northern Pacific Railroad bridge across the Missouri. Above, the bluff rose to a considerable height; below was the end of the spur track, with a flimsy shed serving for the storage of river-bound freight, and riding lazily upon the coffee-colored water of the Missouri were two steamboats tethered to posts set in the bank. Passage for our party had been engaged upon a steamer which had not yet arrived, and we awaited our embarkation in our hillside camp during a week of cold and disconsolate weather, but my spirits were exuberant.

Our tents were sound and serviceable, and we were all experienced campers. There was none of that unhappy discomfort which attends the novice. We had an excellent camp cook and were well supplied with provisions. Our water supply was the matter of most serious moment. The precious fluid could be obtained only from the Missouri River, and the arrival of the first installment from this source was followed by a convention having some of the features of an inquest. We agreed that it was a fluid and that its chief ingredient was water; its color suggested cheap restaurant coffee well diluted with skim milk. It appeared to be rather thick, and this appearance was explained when it had time to settle. We adopted the expedient of keeping our camp supply in two washtubs, using it only after it had stood twenty-four hours. The result was a fluid of milky opaqueness having apparently no other bad qualities.

The boys of our party, and there were three or four of us, tramped over the frozen or muddy ground to the town and back, or on excursions in exploration of the country so strange and interesting. We discovered our first cactus quite accidentally and conducted various experiments for the removal of its spines from our feet. We flushed a few coveys of sage hens and were convinced at first that they were wild turkeys. We inspected with considerable interest the sandstone obelisk which was to mark the scene of Custer's massacre. It lay side-tracked, halfway to its destination, in undignified melancholy at the end of the spur track on the muddy bank of the unlovely river.

The steamers at the bank, much like the river craft with which we were familiar, were no special curiosity to us, but the deck hands on one of them were the first real southern negroes I had ever seen, unbelievably black, unintelligible in speech, creatures to be observed from a respectful distance.

Before the arrival of our steamer, the *Key West,* our floating neighbors had severally departed, pioneering the crooked shallows of the upper Missouri on their way to Fort Benton. One bright but keen and windy day I walked with a companion along the hills down the river, hoping to detect the smoke of our approaching steamer. The river in its narrow valley was fringed with cottonwoods; the sky was clear and indescribably blue; the sun was bright and the eye found nothing in the prospect to justify or explain the cold except the drab and serious aspect of the prairies and the leafless trees. We stood upon a high point, our eyes fatigued with unaccustomed distances. Across the river on the high ground could be seen the frontier outpost, Fort Abraham Lincoln—its flag extended in metal-like rigidity before the unrelenting gale. Here I became fully aware of the changed and foreign aspect of the earth. My boyhood had been spent among forests or in those inconsequential breaches where puny man had forced an opening, through which the sky might be visible. I had hardly seen a sunrise or a sunset in my life, the sky had been for me but an opening in the foliage. Here on the bleak hilltop I felt, more than ever before, unsheltered and naked. But we were too cold for sentiment or any sensation other than numbness, and hurried back to camp with no tidings of our steamer. Next morning, however, we waked to the knowledge that the landing had a new occupant. The *Key West* had arrived. She was a stern wheeler like all other boats plying the upper Missouri.

Our departure was prompt but not hurried. We transferred our effects from camp and hotel to the boat and after a proper amount of confusion and indecision were assigned our quarters, the ladies of the party and the elders in tiny staterooms, while the younger men and boys found sleeping accommodations in double-decked removable cots ranged down the center of the saloon. The boat was crowded with passengers and we were fed in relays. My inspection of the boat was casual, for the mysteries of the unfolding river held a greater charm. Near the ship's bell on the hurricane deck was the post most favored, and on the first day of river travel my vigilance was rewarded by a long survey of the old Mandan village and Lewis and Clark's winter camp of 1804-1805.

CHAPTER III

UP THE RIVER

HE *Key West* was larger than any of the steamboats plying the Chippewa. She was not a new boat and in no sense a clipper, but she was well fitted for the work, well officered and well found, and for more than two weeks was a very comfortable home for us. I managed in some fashion to reach a friendly understanding with the pilots, one a nervous old gentleman about ready for the retired list, the other a man below middle age, imperturbable and well pleased with himself. These autocrats united in a certain contempt for the captain, who was referred to as an "Ohio river man." This term I felt sure was surcharged with opprobrium. My interest in the river lasted for a day or so when it was killed by the monotony.

The Missouri was at a low stage. There was evidence of high water when the ice had gone out with the melted prairie snows, but the weather was still cool and the June rise, that product of warm rains and mountain snows, was a month away. Our little craft threaded its way up the shrunken, muddy stream, following the windings of the river from bluff to bluff in a zigzag course through the narrow wooded valley, hemmed in by the endless, never changing prairies which we sensed, but never saw. We would pass occasionally a solitary tepee, a novel sight to us, so different from the wigwam of the Chippewas. Once in a while Indians on horseback would be glimpsed at the river edge of the prairie, but the river valley itself was bleak and drear.

Our deck hands or roustabouts were Scandinavians. I soon became familiar with them and was *persona grata* in the engine room where I brought into practice my knowledge of the wiper's craft, acquired in the little roundhouse in Chippewa Falls. I had but little spending money and made slight progress in my approaches toward the steward, who presided behind a tiny bar at the forward end of the cabin where he dispensed candies, tobacco, and liquors; nor did I ever penetrate the galley or receive special favors from that quarter. An obsequious devotion to the pilots, however, met with its reward, and I soon had the freedom of that airy palace, the pilot house. I would rescue on occasion an egg from our chicken coop on the hurricane deck, and such eggs soft boiled in a can held precariously under the mud-valve were offered daily to the guiding deities in their lofty lookout.

We made no attempt to run at night. The river was low, we were making the first trip of the season and the untrustworthy stream had made such changes since last year that it was almost like an exploring expedition. At more than one point I was shown where the river had abandoned its bed of the year before and found a new channel miles distant. So we contented ourselves with what progress we could make while daylight served. As we neared the mouth of the Yellowstone we were treated one day to an unmistakable prairie gale. The protection afforded by the highlands that walled the river valley did not avail against the terrific power of this wind. Accustomed as I had been to the sheltered forest, there was something really appalling in its fury and power. Our captain very prudently made fast to the bank under a sheltering bluff and there we idled through the whole day, pelted by leaves and limbs from swaying trees, and sand and dust from the wind-swept plains.

The river was monotonous until the mouth of the Yellowstone was reached. We would be informed occasionally that we were passing the ruins of an ancient trading post or some more modern military outpost. We were in the country of the untamed Sioux, who four years earlier had displayed their cunning and savagery in the de-

We were in the country of the untamed Sioux.

struction of Custer and his troopers. We were within the boundaries of Montana and I felt a growing disappointment with the tameness of the trip. We had seen no wild buffalo, very few Indians, no scouts, no Indian fighters, nothing in fact to bring into reality the highly colored pictures I had painted of the wild West. The woodyard men were no more romantic than the Wisconsin lumbermen. I had not seen a revolver, a buckskin hunting shirt, a scalp, nor even a war bonnet. I hinted my disappointment to the pilots and they assured me I would see many Indians and that when we reached the mouth of the Musselshell, they could show me a very select collection of desperadoes.

When we had passed the mouth of the Yellowstone, our river highway was diminished in volume and noticeably swifter. The country was treeless but no longer flat prairie, and from our steamer we had an occasional glimpse into the weird distance of the Bad Lands and soon reached the country of sandstone cliffs and isolated buttes. Our table was well supplied with elk and buffalo meat and our refrigerator was filled with ice found along the banks of the river, partly covered with sand.

About this time a sense of uneasiness was noticeable in the engine room. Far down the river was visible now and then the smoke of some river steamboat gaining upon us. I never knew, or have forgotten, her name, but for the next week, or until we reached our destination, the pursuing specter haunted us night and day. "Wooding up" was hurried and feverish. We ran at night until we fetched up against something and when we were safely aground on some mud-bank the small boat was launched and the channel sought and sounded by lantern light. Our boat drew but three feet of water, but in many places the river had sprawled itself over a mile of bottom land and divided into numerous channels. More than once we resorted to "sparring," an operation suggesting walking on stilts, and the boat literally dragged herself over bars where the water was not over two feet in depth. Both pilots were in the pilot house most of the time. When a gunny sack was hung over the steam gauge, I knew that we were bound to beat the rival steamboat even though it took unlawful steam pressure to do it. The superstructure trembled constantly with the exertion of the engines and still the smoke of the pursuer was occasionally visible. After a time it seemed that we had outdistanced the competing boat and our pace became less feverish, although we wasted no time.

Day by day we fought the interminable river and our boat hauled herself up two rapids with hawser and capstan, which brought us into a country of fantastic cliffs where dinosaur bones protruded from the rocks.

Indians, the wild Indians of the plains, were now considerably in evidence. I saw my first bull-boat, a basket framework covered with buffalo hide and much resembling a large washtub, and I saw the ludicrous craft in use. The temperature of the spring days was rather crisp and bracing, but the untutored savages displayed a great deal of physical candor, sometimes to the disquiet of the ladies on board. A few times the boat was visited by a select delegation, and small matters of trade were carried on. We saw the semi-hostile Sioux in force at Poplar River and Wolf Point where we unloaded supplies for their benefit. Although the frontier was at peace, these barbarians seemed alert, sullen, and defiant. Many were painted, their ears gashed, and they wore strings of trinkets and trophies around their unlovely necks. One hideous old pirate was decorated with several mummified fingers culled from some ancient enemy. They were altogether an unpleasant lot, and I looked with less contempt upon the stack of Springfield muskets at the forward end of the cabin.

Somewhere near the mouth of the Musselshell while we were making our toilsome way up stream, there suddenly appeared around a bend in the river another steamboat, bound down. She almost literally flashed by us. I hardly had time to make out her name, although I am sure we were not twenty feet apart at meeting. Almost before I could turn my head she had disappeared down the river and was gone. She was a boat that had preceded us by about a week. Her up-river cargo had been discharged and she would retrace in about five days the distance that had taken her more than two weeks to cover traveling up stream.

CHAPTER IV

FORT BENTON TO THE MUSSELSHELL

I N THE upper reaches of the river the scenery was, to my eyes, mountainous. The water was no longer muddy but bright and transparent. We had no serious mishaps and very few delays and at last, one fine bright morning, clambered over Shonkin Bar and, ten miles above it, after much tooting of the whistle, approached the landing at Fort Benton.

The bottom lands south of the river were low and subject to overflow. On the north side, the bank was bluff, and the lively little town was about on a level with our hurricane deck, which gave us a preview of Fort Benton before we tied up. It was less than a town of one street, a town of one side of one street. This street or road ran parallel to the cut bank of the river and not far from it. On the land side of the road there was a string of low buildings, extending from the old adobe fort of the fur traders to a point perhaps a quarter of a mile up stream. I had no serious duties to perform, and while our goods were being discharged and preparations for our overland journey were under way, I explored this river metropolis thoroughly. There were three general stores doing a wholesale and retail business conducted by reputable and aggressive merchants. There were two hotels, a number of blacksmith shops and innumerable saloons and gambling halls.

I was quite familiar with the Wisconsin saloon, but the Montana "deadfall" resembled this no more than Sitting Bull's Sioux resembled our semidomesticated Chippewas. In the first place they were open to the sidewalk, they were filled with card tables or the unfamiliar faro and roulette tables, but what most impressed me was the character and customs of the patrons of the establishments. All of the types of the frontier were to be seen: soldiers, officer and private, steamboat men, the long-haired scout of the Buffalo Bill type, the short-haired cowboy, the shaggy bewhiskered hunter and trapper, Red River half-breeds, full-blooded Indians, the "bull whacker" and the "mule skinner," miners, busted and otherwise, Chinamen, clerks, and professional gamblers. In attire they were kaleidoscopic. Beaded buckskin garments were considerably in evidence and the sombrero seemed standard, though it was not worn to the exclusion of other headgear. The climax of my impressions lay in the realization that almost every man openly, brazenly, carried a monstrous Colt's revolver. It became quite evident that my ethical standards must undergo a change. Not only were the revolvers carried in holsters on great leather belts filled with ammunition, but the weapons occupied a prominent place upon the card tables in front of each player. I waited for some time before one of the gambling saloons for the murder to come off, but grew tired at last and pursued my tour of investigation.

Hardly an hour passed without some novel sight and sound to awake new sensations. I was delighted with everything except the awful profanity that assailed my ears. The men of the Wisconsin woods were suckling babes compared to these frontiersmen. Stage coaches similar to those I had seen in Bismarck came into town regularly from Helena and the mining country to the west. I was in a land of marvels. The streets and alleys were crowded with freight wagons and the prairie behind the town was dotted with the camps of freighters. Twenty to twenty-four oxen made up the usual freight team, yoked to three heavy wagons, larger than any I had ever seen.

I made a very thorough inspection of one of these freight outfits. I was familiar enough with ox yokes, but here were eleven of them in front of the lead wagon, strung like beads upon what I thought was a continuous chain. The wagons were gigantic things, broad gauge, long coupled, with large wheels, and boxes five feet high, above which were arched bows covered with heavy canvas. The second and third wagons had short tongues and were close coupled to the wagon ahead. Each wagon was fitted with a brake mechanism which was an entire novelty to me. On the side of the lead wagon there was a ten-gallon water keg with faucet and cup. Just above it was a long rifle in slings. What aroused my special curiosity was a small Dutch oven, the first I had ever seen, at the camp fire near which the "bull whacker" and a few friends were sitting. My grandmother could have told me the name and the function of this straight-sided squat iron pot, with its flat cover heaped with embers. But while I waited, hoping to have my curiosity satisfied, I listened to the "bull whacker," who was entertaining an audience of five or six who were apparently "pilgrims" like myself. His talk was directed to a visiting "bull whacker," although I cannot but believe the story was intended for our benefit. It was a case of permissive eavesdropping. When the story teller resumed the rôle of cook, the mystery of the Dutch oven was solved, for, after a preliminary squint, the cover was lifted off, disclosing a large, well-baked loaf of bread.

FORT BENTON TO THE MUSSELSHELL

Next day we were ferried across the river and took up our journey southward.

We had found upon our arrival at Fort Benton five or six teams with prairie schooners, in charge of friends who had preceded us to Montana, and in three days after landing were starting on our overland journey to the forks of the Musselshell, one hundred and forty miles distant. We were well equipped and favored with fair weather. The green prairies afforded excellent grazing to our horses; we were unencumbered with cattle and this phase of our emigration was as delightful as our river journey. About ten miles from Fort Benton we came upon a frontiersman beginning a home on a little stream, but from this point we traveled a hundred miles to the east of Square Butte and into the Musselshell Valley without encountering another human being. We followed a faint unauthoritative track. There was no road in the proper sense of the term, no bridges, no grades.

On the second day after leaving Fort Benton, we had camped for noon at a little stream and after the noonday meal I strolled out of camp with a comrade of my own age. We followed the wagon tracks which were leading us around the foot of Square Butte, an immense, isolated, flat-topped outpost of the mountains. We crossed one little hillock and mounted toward the crest of another.

UBET

In a little valley ahead of us, we saw an Indian waving a blanket. Instantly, we dropped prone and discussed the situation. Like true scouts we first looked to our arms. My comrade had a dubious thirty-two-caliber revolver, using short rim-fire cartridges, of which he had three only. It was almost as effective as no weapon at all. My bowie knife was hung in its scabbard from a suspender button and I had my little twenty-two-caliber seven shooter, with five cartridges. It was not a weapon, it could only be classed as an irritant. The frontal attack was discredited with us, and we decided that a flank movement might be decisive. Accordingly we crawled cautiously around the point of a hill and discovered two work horses with harness on, grazing in the creek bottom, and a woman standing up in a lumber wagon, shaking dust out of a laprobe. It was true that her small bonnet carried two stiffly militant feathers, but from our flank position she did not at all resemble a "scourge of the settlements." The campers were attached to our party for the sake of company on the long drive and had merely pushed ahead a quarter of a mile, looking for better grass. Whenever I feel urged to criticize a youth for lack of judgment or for sheer foolishness, I remember this imbecility and become tolerant, even sympathetic.

At Arrow Creek we had to make the ascent to

Arrow Creek . . . the northerly rim of the Judith Basin.

the northerly rim of the Judith Basin up the infamous Arrow Creek hill, a distance of only four miles, but over a jumble of detached buttes and hillocks, too steep to be flanked. We hauled our wagons with doubled teams to the top of each elevation (a frontal attack in each case) then let them down with rough-locked wheels to the foot of the hill (the beginning of the next ascent) where the operation was repeated.

This was the only serious barrier on our road and when it was surmounted almost our whole course across the Judith Basin to the Gap, some seventy miles distant, was visible. Here for the first time I began to sense the real meaning of the mountains and prairies. Nine or ten mountain ranges, detached bulwarks of the Rockies, were in view, some distant and unreal, others close at hand, stark and palpable. These were for the eye. Under foot, close at hand, was the comfort of the firm-sodded, sloping benchland, the rolling hills and the pleasant infrequent water-courses. Prairie fires had destroyed the old grass, but the warm sun of spring had already covered the ground with the most brilliant green. Three lovely spring days in this setting gave me the beginning of that intimate sense of fellowship with this foothill empire which was never to leave me.

We had the usual troubles in fording the various

streams that crossed our trail. Our hunters found game enough to keep us supplied with meat. We adopted the precaution, perhaps unnecessary, of keeping armed guards at night, but saw no Indians, hostile or otherwise.

When we were within four miles of Judith Gap we struck the old Carroll Trail and there I saw the beginnings of Ubet, for in 1879 my father, visualizing the rapid settlement of the Judith Basin, had built a claim cabin intending to establish a road ranch. About a month before our arrival, two travelers camping at this spot for the night were caught in a fierce spring blizzard and being stormbound for three or four days had burned the cabin bit by bit to keep from freezing to death. Four miles beyond, at the easternmost point of the Belt Mountains, D. A. Meagher was building a cabin, and a mile beyond it Al Stephens was established in anticipation of coming trade. At Robert's Creek we were met by a team sent from my father's camp at the sawmill site in the Belt Mountains. Here, in company with four others, I left the party and that night was in council with my father whom I had not seen for more than a year.

The last stage of our journey from the Saw-mill Gulch was about thirty miles, but we were traveling light with a tough little team of cayuses and a lumber wagon almost empty. The day was bright and warm and our course lay over thinly grassed uplands, dipping into an occasional insignificant watercourse. Early in the afternoon from the top of a sterile hill, west of Daisy Dean, I beheld my destination, a huddle of diminutive log cabins at the foot of a low hill near the confluence of two small streams. We were at the head of the Mussel-shell Valley. Mountains fronted and flanked us; mountains naked and snowy; mountains rounded and green; old mountains revealing rocky vertebrae. From the contemplation of these encompassing heights the eye turned incredulous to the little smudge of civilization in the midst of the untouched wilderness.

CHAPTER V

MY NEW ABODE

I PRESUME THAT the greater part of an hour was consumed after our arrival in renewing acquaintances with my mother and younger brother and sister, after which I took steps to explore my new surroundings. The settlement was housed in a four-room log cabin, L shaped, with a dirt roof. One end room was the trading post. Next to this was the bunk house where the regular employees and transients slept, called the "ram pasture." The corner room was our family bedroom. Connecting with it, forming the short end of the L, was a combination kitchen and dining room. This room was distinguished because it was the only one having a board floor. There were two other log buildings, a stable which would accommodate about four animals, and a dugout storehouse and root-cellar.

The door to the trading post was so low that, perhaps without necessity, I ducked my head in entering. I had no sooner entered than I felt the place was crowded. A card table surrounded by four poker players took up almost every foot of available floor space. The game must have been interesting, or I must have been uninteresting, for almost no attention was given to my entrance. This inattention to myself was in no sense reciprocal, for the emporium with its meager display of merchandise was ignored while I studied the men at the table.

Facing me was "Antelope" Charlie, a tall well-built young man with long hair and the mustache and goatee so much affected by the scout. His legs were under the table, but there was visible above it a gorgeously decorated buckskin shirt of Indian manufacture. At his right sat a famous frontier character, carrying easily the name of "Liver-eating" Johnson. He was a big, broad, burly man, unkempt and abundantly bearded. His flannel overshirt as well as his red flannel undershirt was negligently unbuttoned. His hairy arms and big hands suggested the sailor. Opposed to him I saw my first specimen of the squawman, Jim Carpenter. In this brotherhood Carpenter had taken the highest degree, for he was not only allied to a squaw, but he had modified both costume and appearance to conform as nearly as possible to the savage standard. He was a smooth-faced, middle-aged Missourian. His rather scanty hair was worn long, the ridiculously thin side-braids with their decorations of fur and trumpery ornaments hanging before his ears. He wore a fancy buckskin hunting shirt and a leather belt, which with its dependent knife sheath was heavily decorated with brass studs. Sitting with his back towards me was Frank Gaugler, the owner of the establishment. It was some time before the rigor of the game relaxed and my advent was noticed, whereupon I was accorded words of welcome and an opportunity to meet my future employer. He was a man of medium size, kindly and honest, but not aggressive.

The room was small for its purpose, not more than twelve by sixteen feet. Across one end was a crude bar or counter and piled upon rough shelves behind this was a scant but varied showing of the general stock. A few bottles of Hostetter's and Angostura with one or two cordials were tucked on a shelf within view, but of the most active commodity, whiskey, no advertisement was necessary. Strictly speaking the stock display was inartistic. Some showy trinkets for Indian trade hung from nails, and the shelves were tightly packed with "sour-dough" clothing.

For something more than two months I took a minor part in the life at the forks of the Musselshell. The tide of emigration from the settlements in the older valleys west of us was commencing. There was considerable travel and life was active and full of business. At first I had no regular employment, although I made myself useful in the trading post, especially at those times when the proprietor was incapacitated by liquor. I took a kindergarten course and was able to ride to our post office, Martinsdale, something more than a half mile distant and make a safe return. In the absence of any other help, I assisted my mother in her kitchen work and rapidly accommodated myself to the new environment.

Game was plentiful and our community at that time subsisted almost entirely on meat. One morning while I was helping my mother wash the breakfast dishes, Bob Carpenter appeared at the door and my mother said to him in the most matter-of-fact way, "Bob, I am about out of meat. I wish you would get me something nice for dinner."

"All right, ma'am," said Bob, and soon disappeared over the little hill back of the house with his rifle on his arm. Our dish-washing operations were not concluded when I heard two shots in succession, and twenty minutes later our hunter appeared at the door with an antelope across his shoulders.

We had for visitors at this time a family of Red River half-breeds who camped near us for a month or so, and I became quite intimate with the son and heir of this clan, Moses Wells, who was about my own age. Beyond the fact that he could ride and shoot, was an accomplished hunter and could speak English, French, and three or four Indian languages fluently, he was uneducated. After one hunting trip with him, I sat at his feet and confessed myself ignorant of everything essential. We started early one bright morning for the mountains some twelve miles distant, each mounted on a reliable saddle horse, and cantered over the smiling prairies until we were within a couple of miles of the timber line. We were upon the high ground between Daisy Dean and Mud creeks and here a careful survey of the foothills discovered to Moses a large band of black-tail deer. After considerable difficulty I managed to see them too. Up to this time I had assumed that this hunting expedition was a joint affair. I now accepted gracefully a subordinate position which I never lost. The trained eye of the half-breed instantly discovered the weakness of the position held by the deer, and we left the eminence and galloped in a devious course through coulees and low ground until it became necessary to change our mode of travel. Tying our horses to some stunted willows we hurried forward on foot, then on all fours, and I remember that this part of the approach was through the snowy slush of a ravine. Next, prone on our faces in the grass, we wormed our way to a position behind a prostrate tree. Here I was informed in a subdued whisper that there were about fifty blacktail deer quite close to us and I meekly complied with the suggestion that we should exchange guns. (Until the exchange I had the better arm.) I was directed to get ready and fire at will as soon as my companion had fired the first shot, but when I lifted my head so that the game was visible, I was stricken with a virulent attack of buck fever and fired but one shot. (The bullet may be found by anyone who chops down the right tree and spilts it into kindling wood.) But the hunt was not a total failure, for the uneducated half-breed with twelve cartridges in the magazine of my '73 Winchester had killed nine large deer. Our unequal achievements, together with the fact that my horse bucked me off on my ride homeward, had a tendency to reduce my self-esteem to proper proportions. I made one more excursion with Moses, but on this occasion we flagged antelope and I was the flag. I took my position as directed by my comrade and there, lying on my back, I waved my legs in the air for what seemed an interminable time. The antelope were attracted by this ridiculous behavior and three of them remained as testimonials to the skill of the sixteen-year-old half-breed.

I was not entirely discouraged by my questionable success as a hunter, but went out one day on a solo hunt with a borrowed gun. Mounting a hill not far from home, I had a choice of several small bands of antelope and in a careful imitation of my half-breed friend, was so successful in stalking the selected group that I soon found myself lying behind a sheltering bunch of grass and sage within a hundred yards of my unsuspecting victims. There was no occasion for hurry and I felt a consoling calm with an entire absence of buck fever, but out of my inexperience I foolishly elevated the sights on my rifle and the only result of my ineffectual fusillade was a small tuft of antelope hair which drifted on the breeze for a few yards before settling to earth. It may be fairly said that this ended my career as a hunter. I was thoroughly discouraged and disgusted and from this time forward I professed a distaste for the sport which was far from real.

My little pocket pistol was so provocative of mirth that it was soon discarded, and as it seemed quite necessary that I should be armed with a six-shooter I managed to equip myself with the abandoned armament of a tenderfoot. This weapon I carried in an improvised holster for about two days, or until I was disarmed by my mother.

CHAPTER VI

I DECIDE TO GO COWBOY

FROM the moment of my arrival at my new home I was conscious of the desirability, amounting almost to necessity, of conforming to the new customs and standards. It was true that I had changed only from one frontier to another, but the *mores* were widely different. Our section of Montana was socially in a state of flux. The trader, hunter, and trapper were in evidence, but their day was waning; the farmer had not yet appeared. Sheepmen and cattlemen were driving their herds into the country, but neither their costumes nor their customs were then standardized. There was no Indian war and the remnants of the clan of scout plainsmen were thin and unconvincing.

I was as imitative as a monkey, but my ideals fluctuated and I hardly knew what to imitate. My father, whom I saw occasionally, was busied in his sawmill enterprise and preserved with considerable integrity the traditions of the Wisconsin woods, convicting himself of a conservatism I could not emulate. So I continued in my uncertainty until the Musselshell round-up, for one feverish day, pervaded our settlement. In those days the round-up was not homogeneous, but there was a leaven in it of the real cowboy, the Texas type at that time prevailing, and from that day I knew what I wanted to be. I was quite unable to decide upon any one individual for my model, my choice wavering between Sim Roberts, Ike Morgan, and John Cabler, but from them I drew and idealized a type, something to be striven for but never attained. My interest in the trading post vanished with the departure of the round-up. The half-breed influence became a thing of the past. I still enjoyed the companionship of my half-breed chum and Sidonie, his sister (who helped my mother in the kitchen), dark and half wild, padding about in her moccasins—a galvanized savage, but their real influence had faded.

I had no saddle and was hardly content to be continually borrowing, so I chaffered with the matron of the half-breed family and she made me a Red River saddle, that queer contrivance conforming to the half-breed's idea of what a saddle should be, a buckskin pad stuffed with antelope hair, shaped like and somewhat resembling a monstrous, elongated doughnut. This affair was strapped to the horse's back by a surcingle, and from the surcingle two small iron stirrups depended. I was never entirely satisfied with this saddle, but it was several months before I obtained title, more or less questionable, to a cheap rig of the cowboy type, which served me for a year and a half. Now came my opportunity. A "bull-whacker" on his way to Cow Island was taken sick in our vicinity and I was engaged to herd his cattle, twenty-four work oxen. For this service I was given use of his pony and riding gear and paid a dollar a day. I prayed for his lingering illness, though he was scarcely two weeks disabled, but by the time he had recovered I considered myself a properly qualified cowboy.

My father was having difficulty at the sawmill, which was not surprising, in view of the fact that the nearest machine shop was one hundred and fifty miles distant and nothing but minor repairs could be made on the spot. As nothing could be done towards the building of a new home until the saw-mill ventures was successful, we were naturally interested in father's occasional visits or the news gathered from other sources. A handy man employed at the sawmill had come to our place with a small load of lumber, the first fruits of the new enterprise, and we pumped him dry during his short stay. His exciting piece of news concerned the poisoning of the Wilson twins. His account as I remember it follows:

"You know there was me and John Sunday, the 'bull whacker.' He was hauling logs, and Ernie Allis, he was mostly playing the flute and reading novels; and there was Wilson, the blacksmith, and Mrs. Wilson and the Wilson twins, Hayes and Wheeler, they are about four years old. We call them 'Wheeze Inhalor,' whenever we want to stir up Mrs. Wilson. She is awfully fussy and particular about grammar and such things. I remember one day she was complaining about being so fat and she said when she was married her burst measure was just thirty-six inches.

"Ernie had taken the saddle horse and his rifle and a novel and had gone up the gulch to a park where our work teams used to graze. Sunday and Wilson had helped me roll up a log on the house I was building and I was at work notching the next log, when Sunday came running from Ernie's tent all excited and het up. He ran right up to Wilson and his wife and began to stutter and wave his arms. He is the most ornamental stutterer I ever knew. He said, 'Hack, hack, hack,' and then he choked and gargled and swallowed and rolled his eyes and then he grabbed Wilson by the arm and started running for the tent with me and Mrs. Wilson right behind him and there we did find a mess.

"Ernie had a beautiful black walnut chest all

filled with little glass bottles of homeopathic specifics, and Hayes and Wheeler had busted into it and were eating the little white pills by the handful and the ruin was pretty complete. There were empty bottles all over the ground and on the blankets. Of course we were in hopes that they hadn't got any poison, but the first empty bottle I got hold of was strychnine, and the next was belladonna, and Mrs. Wilson drew one labeled 'Arsenicum Album' and she began to yell bloody murder. Wilson had an empty bottle in his hand that was called 'Nux Vomica' and he just squatted there and looked at the durn thing and said, 'Glory, glory!' They didn't seem to have any sense at all. I said to John, 'Run over to the house and see if you can find some mustard,' and I grabbed Hayes or Wheeler, I don't know which, and stuck my finger down his throat and I said to Wilson, 'We've just naturally got to make them puke that stuff up.' So he began poking his finger down the other twin's throat, but we didn't fetch anything. Then John came back with a can of allspice. Mrs. Wilson was just sobbing and screaming, but Wilson was willing to do anything. He kept saying, 'Glory, glory!' but he upended his kid and tried to shake out the poison, but all he got was a kick in the eye.

"Then I got an idea and I began scrambling through the bottles to see if I could find an emetic.

In about a minute I said, 'Hurrah, they're all right!' for I found a bottle of ipecacuanha and it was plumb empty. 'They're all right,' said I, 'they are poisoned, but they took the antidote too. There is going to be an eruption in about a minute.' Mrs. Wilson was sobbing, but she says, 'Did they both take it?' That stumped me and I ran over to the cabin and looked around for the nastiest stuff I could find. There was a cup of bacon grease that didn't look very wholesome and I poured in some castor oil that I knew was rancid and back I went on the jump and we began to stuff those kids with the mixture. We didn't get much down, and Hayes, or maybe it was Wheeler, bit my finger, but when we got through we had smeared them up so that if they could have seen themselves they would have vomited all right. Then I got another good idea. I said to John, 'Hook onto the lumberwagon and we'll take them down to Al Stephens' place, maybe he has something.' So we all piled into the lumberwagon, Mr. and Mrs. Wilson and the two kids in the seat, and John started the cattle down the gulch on the lope. Funny thing, he never stuttered when he was talking to the cattle. We just tore down the gulch. We must have been making nearly four miles an hour and it was only three miles to Stephens' trading post, but just as we got out of the gulch onto the grass land we ran

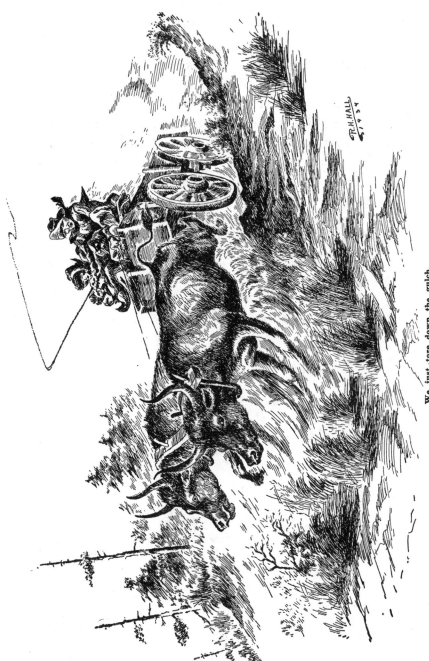

We just tore down the gulch.

slam into a bunch of buffalo, about fifty head I should judge, and behind them were four or five Blackfeet on their buffalo ponies. Of course our cattle couldn't keep up, but they tried their darnedest and away we went, exactly where we didn't want to go and we never stopped until we hit a coulee, when the cattle broke loose from the wagon and left us there in a heap.

"Nobody was hurt, and before John got back with the cattle, the kids were chasing grasshoppers and picking flowers. All the poison they had swallowed hadn't made them turn a hair and when we got back to camp, Mrs. Wilson washed them up and they looked as good as new."

CHAPTER VII

I ACCEPT A POSITION

THE summer was full of incident and excitement to me; there was novelty in everything. The very skins and pelts over which I sweated in the baling press, were fraught with romance as well as strange odors, and the men who brought them were as strange and romantic as their commodities —half-breed peddlers, drifting from tribe to tribe and picking up chance bargains; solitary trappers, coming in after six months' sojourn in the hills. Occasionally some lone Indian with the dawning of a commercial instinct would come in with his peltries and spend a day purchasing merchandise that he could carry away in one hand. A sample purchase from such a customer would comprise ten pounds of flour, two pounds of brown sugar, forty cartridges, a butcher knife, a small tin-backed mirror and perhaps a pair of tweezers to pull out the unwelcome whisker, never omitting a small quantity of tobacco. This he would purchase in the regular way of trade, but the real joy of the occasion to him would be the attempt to get some whiskey, taboo by the laws of God and man.

The prices charged at Gaugler's establishment were exorbitant. Hardly anything was sold for less than one hundred per cent above cost and the profit on some articles was nothing less than outrageous. This could be explained in part by the fact that the current coin of the lowest denomination was the twenty-five-cent piece, "two bits." The popular little mirrors cost two and a half cents, clay pipes about the same, but they were sold for twenty-five cents each. Such profits, added to the expense of transportation by the long river trip and the slow-moving ox trains, made the cost to the customer almost prohibitive, so we made a virtue of necessity, doing without many things that in a civilized community would be considered indispensable. Lard and all pork products were shipped in and were luxuries. Kerosene in five-gallon tins was an imported article as far as we were concerned, and our common light was a candle, home-made from buffalo tallow. The plutocrats might purchase the tinned fruit of the period, but for the most of us there were only old-fashioned dried apples and peaches. We had no butter and substituted a variety of rich gravies.

The activities of this summer of 1880 appeared to me somewhat feverish, but I discovered that winter was regarded as a hibernating period and everything to be done must be accomplished in the short, fierce summer. Gaugler had undertaken the erection of a real store building. The new building had a cellar underneath its puncheon floor and boasted the first shingle roof in the Musselshell Valley. Its dimensions were about sixteen by twenty-two feet and it was heated by a stove. At odd times I assisted at this work, sometimes going to the mountains with the men for logs or acting as volunteer assistant to the carpenters and others. My other employments were various; my duties were not arduous. I was made messenger on many occasions and became reasonably familiar with the country at the head of the valley and quite at home in the saddle.

The valley below us and the Judith Basin were inviting the stockmen from the older settled sections of Montana and our little settlement was occasionally enlivened by the arrival of a herd of cattle or a band of sheep on trail to new ranges. With one of these parties there came a boy of about my own age, fresh from Missouri, and in the shy and peculiar way of youth, here began the acquaintance between myself and Charley Russell, later known as the "Cowboy Artist."

It was at that time too that I had my first intimate glimpse of the United States Army on the frontier. For three years, or since Looking Glass and Chief Joseph with their Nez Percés had crossed our country, there had been no Indian outbreak, but some military force had been maintained at the various frontier posts or forts as they were called. Preliminary work, looking towards the establishment of Fort Maginnis east of the Judith Mountains, was under way, and our settlement, which had taken the name of Martinsdale after our newly established post office, was headquarters for a company of "mounted infantry." This contradiction in terms was the result of the endless struggle between red tape, the most rigid material known to science, and the necessities of the occasion. An infantryman proper in pursuit of marauding Indians was about as effective as a cast iron dog in pursuit of a jack rabbit. Our army, proportioned on obsolete models, was strong in the infantry arm. Cavalrymen were needed from Mexico to Canada and of those there was a great dearth, so, by some departmental ruling or other jugglery, "the mounted infantryman" was created and, like most special creations, was somewhat freakish, but he served.

My inconsiderable part in the events of this period was preparing me for my first real adventure, and this adventure was moving slowly and relentlessly in my direction. It had the shape and substance of a herd of cattle on the trail to new pastures in the buffalo country. In an effort to fix the time of its arrival, I recall that one day early in August two men, with the cradles known to our ancestors, went into the field to harvest the oats (a full three acres) and were driven to shelter by a violent snow squall. I had hardly ceased marveling at this display of Montana climate before one of the DHS herds reached our settlement shorthanded and I "accepted a position" as cowboy at thirty dollars a month. There was a wild scramble to get together the equipment available for my new rôle, and that afternoon I was happy in the humblest position, behind the "drag" of a herd of fifteen hundred stock cattle.

There were about twelve of us in the party. Besides the foreman there was the cook, who drove the mess wagon, and two night herders, who slept in a very primitive Pullman on a bed suspended from the bows of the calf wagon. Below them in the body of the wagon was the nursery for those inopportune calves dropped in the course of the day, or too tired to follow the herd. This combination was hauled by a dignified and solemn yoke of oxen and was in charge of a lank youth who was much inclined to follow the example of the night herders and sleep in his seat. The post of honor was held, of course, by the two men on opposite sides, who directed the head or "point" of the herd. Next in importance was the pair working perhaps a quarter of a mile behind them, on the "flank" and three or four followed in the rear, urging along what was called the "drag" or "dragtail," the discouraged or unambitious dregs of the herd, old bulls, the footsore and the weary, and young calves. All this I learned in five miles' travel, before we camped for the night on Daisy Dean.

My joy in my new employment was somewhat tempered by the consciousness that I was considered in my true character, a tenderfoot, a "pilgrim," a kid, picked up to fill as nearly as possible a place made vacant by the defection of a real cowboy. I discovered that camp fare was bountiful but not elaborate, that my bed was hardly as comfortable as that to which I had been accustomed, also that we were expected to roll out of our blankets at a painfully early hour each morning. Much I had to learn and some of this knowledge was only acquired after years of effort, but the fundamentals were easily understood. I was to get up promptly when called, to dress with alacrity, to roll my meager bed into a compact bundle, tie it securely, and deposit it in the mess wagon. I was automatically penalized if I left anything lying around loose when we moved camp. It was a part of every man's duty to assist in taking down the tent and stowing it properly, as well as in all other work not within the cook's jurisdiction. There was also a horse to be caught and saddled.

Much of this work was done in the half light of dawn and before breakfast. This finished and the sun not yet risen, we were in our saddles and on our way to relieve the two night herders who had held the herd during the night. On this morning in particular, the cattle had left the bed ground and were strung out for nearly a mile, grazing in the anxious and hurried manner usual at that time of day. Our route, almost to our destination, lay along the disused Carroll Trail. For nearly forty miles I was returning over ground covered on my journey from Fort Benton, but there was a new interest in the experience. I was appraising my companions and being subjected to some measure of scrutiny on their part. I learned their names and nicknames and collected information more or less reliable concerning their histories and antecedents. We could be called cowboys only by courtesy. There were four or five men somewhat experienced in handling cattle, two or three glorified farm hands, and the rest, like myself, were green boys or casual laborers.

Our task was not a difficult one. The herd was "trail broke" and somewhat footsore, the country was open, unfenced, unstocked, and we saw no buffalo except at a distance. We were driving through a well-watered region of virgin pastures and it was only necessary to keep our cattle grazing in the general direction desired, with some reference to mid-day water. It might almost be said that we had the world to ourselves. On the third day we passed a small camp of Indians with no exchange of either hostilities or civilities. It was early morning, clear and chill, but the young men of the tribe were stirring, clad in moccasins, belts, and breech cloths, possibly goose flesh, while we were bundled in our coats and heavy clothing. As our herd descended the long slope to the Ubet Valley, I could see the blackened site of my father's claim cabin, and as an evidence of continued possessory intent, a crop of hay had been harvested and neatly stacked.

In the Judith Gap there came to our camp one night a buckskin-attired scout of the long-haired variety, who abode with us until after breakfast and told marvelous stories of disaster, due in every instance to failure to follow his advice. We were passed by a paymaster and his escort en route to Fort Maginnis, then in course of construction, and when near our destination, we, in turn, passed a train of bull teams.

To a sixteen-year-old boy there was a humdrum

quality in the work, after the first novelty had worn off, but those of us incompetents in the dusty rear of the road were not without resource and we managed to diversify our work in ways not always orthodox. Our ropes were constantly in motion and if our road had been a thousand miles longer we might have become lasso experts. As it was some skill was developed and the small laggards were thoroughly halter broken.

On one hot day, the foreman and our straw boss had gone ahead to look for water, leaving us with an inert and immovable herd on a dry benchland. One of the boys found a soldier's overcoat in almost complete disrepair, and this garment was modishly arranged upon a large calf. When the surprised animal was released, his demeanor was entirely changed, and from one of the slowest of our deadheads he was transformed into something demoniac. With elevated tail and protruding tongue, giving voice to the most astounding bellows, he charged through the center of the herd, transmitting to them by some strange alchemy his own fervor. In a moment some of us were undergoing a new experience. We were riding pell-mell after a stampeded herd, and thus we rode for a mile or more, the ground trembling, the air filled with the thunderous bellowing of frightened cattle, until the

From one of the slowest of our deadheads he was transformed into something demoniac.

maddened herd poured over the brow of a steep hill into the narrow valley of Beaver Creek. This was a wonderful sight to see, but not more wonderful than the celerity with which our foreman and his right-hand man mounted their horses and fled from impending destruction. The herd was checked in the valley, and, after milling twenty minutes or so, the innocent cause of the stampede was removed and the herd settled back to comparative quiet. Then began the search for two perfectly good pairs of boots and socks, for our superior officers had been surprised while enjoying a footbath. To this day, who put the coat on the calf remains a mystery.

No reasonable complaint could be lodged against those in authority in our party, but rebellion is latent, and anything that tended to the discomfiture of the boss was more or less openly welcomed. On one dark and threatening night there was some uneasiness in the herd, and the boss, moved by some natural anxiety, left his bed, lighted a lantern and, leaving it hung in the tent, went outside to listen. After he had been gone for some minutes one of the boys blew out the lantern. Presently we heard a shout which remained unanswered, only to be followed by more shouts, growing fainter, intermixed with language pungent and objurgatory.

UBET

A cold rain set in and was still falling at dawn when our dripping and exasperated superior found camp. How the lantern went out became another of those inexplicable mysteries of early days.

Near the present site of Lewistown, we left the Carroll Trail and crossed Big Spring Creek not far from a trading-post conducted by a Frenchman. Just above the crossing was the establishment of Reed and Bowles. I might have more to say about these pioneer merchants but for a mishap which gave me something else to think about.

Our cattle were put across the stream in leisurely fashion, and, after crossing the last animal, I found myself in a bend of the creek where my horse was disinclined to enter the stream. It was a case where the horse was wiser than his rider. The stream was crystalline clear, the water appeared to be no more than a foot deep, but when I had spurred my reluctant horse from the grassy bank into the water, it was a case of total immersion, for the horse fell down, and I scrambled out of a pool that was fully three feet deep.

That night we camped on the high ground between the Judith and the Snowy Mountains and I nearly froze because much of my clothing was damp and I was the odd man of our party, unable to double beds with anyone. On the following morning we descended from the country of sparse pines to one of the branches of McDonald Creek and, turning northward, drove our herd over many hills, crossing many streams. Here we narrowly avoided a small war with some "bull-whackers" who were "doubling up" on a steep hill. As we crawled slowly past them we urged our herd with the usual prolonged shouts of "*Oh*-ma-ha-" and "*I*-da-*ho*-o-" The well-trained oxen responded by stopping whenever the emphasis was placed on the "O." We passed on with a consciousness of mischief well performed and also more or less authentic information about our antecedents and our final destination.

This day at our noon camp we were visited by three hungry Indians. The word hungry is perhaps surplusage, for Indians are always hungry. Donations of food were prohibited by our foreman, and those of us who were soft-hearted suffered under compulsion of eating a hearty meal under the wolfish eyes of these savages. There was some retaliation, however, for the Indians almost in our camp killed an antelope and sat down to a nauseating feast of raw liver and entrails, garnished with brains and cracked marrow bones; when they had finished there remained little of the antelope and less of our compassion.

The following day was devoted to branding calves born during the exodus, and signalized my introduction to "calf wrestling." I nearly fainted from horror when the hot iron was applied to the first calf, but I revived with a whiff of the acrid smoke and a sharp prod from the immature horns. Our work was done in a corral, close to a clump of quaking asps, within a few hundred yards of the present site of Giltedge, later a flourishing mining camp.

When we were under way on the morning of the next day we met with an example of Indian vigilance. Upon the top of a rounded butte, two or three miles ahead, there rose a lone Indian, who with his blanket made many semaphoric signals and then faded from view. This was a wireless advice to his camp, perhaps three miles distant, and resulted in a visit from fifteen or twenty Blackfeet, sociable and crudely commercial.

We were within sight of the new buildings of Fort Maginnis and within a mile of the DHS home ranch when we said goodbye to our bovine companions and left them, no longer to be harassed by us, but to face the perils of a new range, hungry wolves and Indians, and a desperately hard winter.

CHAPTER VIII

I MAKE FRIENDS WITH
THE PIEGANS

THE home ranch of the DHS was on Ford Creek. Black Butte, the eastern buttress of the Judiths, was at our north, and the Judiths proper, like an encircling arm, constituted our western and northwestern horizon. This location was an open, fertile, well-watered valley. The streams were bordered by a dense growth of willows, with occasional cottonwoods of good size. Near a beautiful spring there had been constructed a commodious log cabin, L-shaped, and just below it a stockade corral of heavy logs, formed in part by log buildings, quarters for the men and horses. The buildings were provided with loop-holes for defensive purpose and were so placed that all sides of the corral were commanded. The massive hewn doors swung on wooden hinges and could be firmly fastened by heavy wooden latches. We soon made ourselves at home in the men's cabin and scraped acquaintance with earlier arrivals, exchanging experiences on the trail and apocryphal anecdotes of personal history. My sojourn at the ranch was extended for some forgotten reason to two or three weeks, the busiest leisure of my life.

Quite near us there was a camp of fifty lodges of Piegans or Blackfeet Indians under Chief Running Rabbit. They were near the eastern frontier of their vaguely defined territory, and somewhat apprehensive of their savage neighbors. Their camp was so attractive to me that I could hardly be relied upon even at mealtime in the cook-house. I was interested in everything I saw, the decorated tepees, the old ones, begrimed with smoke and travel-stained, with faded effigies and symbols, the new ones, spic and span and glaring; the domestic occupations and home industries, tanning of skins, making of pemmican, preparing winter clothing, plain and ceremonial, the painting of buffalo robes for personal wear, every sight was a new page in my book of experiences.

The typical tepee was a conical lodge of specially tanned elk or buffalo skins stretched over a framework of perhaps twenty-four slim poles of peeled lodge-pole pine. The bottom of the tepee was held down by stones. The door was a slit opening, covered in bad weather by a shield-shaped flap. Within this circular interior with its ever present smoldering fire and simmering kettle, the tent wall was ingeniously wainscoted to a height of three or four feet with tanned buckskin held in place by willow wands tied to the lodge poles. Tanned robes served as beds, and the lord of the lodge reclined luxuriously upon a back-rest covered with a selected pelt.

I was a visitor, tolerated if not welcomed in many tepees. I could not be voluble, for these Indians had little or no English. I knew nothing of the sign language and had only two or three words of Chinook jargon, but my eyes were always open, and through these my youthful curiosity was measurably satisfied. Without fully appreciating it at the time I was enjoying an opportunity to study the Plains Indians, almost unspoiled by civilization. This people had been in contact with the trader for fifty years and had forsaken primitive weapons for the more effective arms of the white man. They had cultivated a taste for some of the foods unknown to their ancestors and clamored for the whiskey occasionally to be had from outlaw traders. Yet, generally speaking, they depended, as had their forbears, upon the native products of their bleak prairies and isolated mountains, the wild game so plentiful and the scanty fruit. They were still in the age of barter. One of my companions tried in vain to purchase a pony for a five dollar bill. The paper symbol was examined with great gravity and earnestness by the Indians and their advisers and handed back with a negative sign, but the purchase was arranged quite promptly for three silver dollars.

I formed a close alliance with two Indian boys of about my own age, Neetah and Tsipah. I fed them surreptitiously but bountifully and to this day am not ashamed of my pilferings. I taught them a few useful words of English and in turn acquired an equal number from their vocabulary. They were fleeter of foot than I, but less successful in wrestling bouts. As their guest I visited their portable homes, but managed to resist dinner invitations. I found, much to my surprise, that the unspoiled Indian at home was not the taciturn savage of romance. The camp was alive with merriment. There was much skylarking and laughter, innocent practical jokes were the rule, and a good deal of hilarity seemed to be based upon a play of words. This unconscious air of gaiety and good fellowship would be thrown off instantly and the whole camp take on a dignity and solemn stateliness upon the arrival of unexpected or unwelcome guests, as the visit of an officer or unsympathetic civilian. The squaws would cease their crooning songs, the play of the children would come to an end, the bucks would become wooden and frigid, and one could almost say that the papooses felt the change in the camp atmosphere. From this I am inclined to generalize and assert that our ideas of taciturnity of the primitive Indians are misconceptions.

I returned home in a lumber wagon drawn by four horses, in company with several others, who, like myself, had been paid off at the end of the drive. I delivered my hoarded wages to my mother and from that moment assumed a matured responsibility as a provider. On the day after my return I was sent with a message to a ranch about fifteen miles distant and thus missed an opportunity to join in a buffalo chase. A small band of buffalo almost invaded our settlement and were pursued by the mobile population. Returning from my errand, I found one melancholy buffalo calf, made captive by a visiting cowboy, and a considerable supply of buffalo meat. At that time we paid no attention to buffalo hides except the tanned robes which we purchased from the Indians.

Any disappointment I might have felt on account of the buffalo chase was lost in the good news that during my absence my mother had found employment for me with two young men who had purchased a band of sheep in a western valley and were then on their way to receive the sheep and drive them into the Judith Basin. My employers had proceeded on their way, and I made a night ride to overtake them at Hall's Ranch. It was understood that I was to be provided not only with food and shelter, but bedding. I was well cared for at Hall's, and the next day we made a hard drive and ended our journey after dark at the sheep ranch west of Fort Logan. Here also was good entertainment.

CHAPTER IX

I CHAPERON A BAND
OF SHEEP

ON THE following day I was taken to the herder's camp at some distance from the home ranch and had my first experience with what was called in later days, a "crazy sheep herder." This individual with whom I was quartered was a man about thirty-five years of age, unkempt, dirty, and disreputable, a man of incessant cackling talk and furtive unsteady eyes. His cabin was filthy and cluttered with worthless gleanings. The only respectable thing about the place was his dog. I found this unwholesome hermit short of provisions, his bacon rusty and unpalatable, his tea undrinkable, and his fried rice too plainly showing the contributions from marauding mice. By bedtime my happiness was somewhat tempered by a growing appreciation of my environment. Our sleep was broken by a visit from a grizzly bear, who frolicked for an hour or so in the corral with the unhappy sheep. The herder contented himself with firing his rifle three or four times in the direction of Ursa

Major. In the morning we found the corral broken and the sheep scattered through the valley, excepting fourteen dead and mangled, some partly consumed in the corral.

After a wholly unsatisfactory breakfast, we gathered the scattered sheep and drove them slowly to the home ranch, where good food and a decent bed effaced the memory of hardship. Here I put in one long, strenuous day chasing sheep through a chute for counting and marking, and even now I have hardly freed my lungs from the acrid dust of that day. The sun had not risen the next morning when I started with my "crazy" friend and two thousand imbecile sheep on the long journey. This was a pedestrian tour and I was wearing my first pair of high-heeled cowboy boots. The morning was clear and crisp and my overcoat was a very welcome part of my equipment. Near Fort Logan our patrons passed us in their new bright spring wagon, and as I was carrying my overcoat by that time, I welcomed the opportunity to deliver it to them.

While the herder went to Fort Logan to purchase food for our midday meal, I kept the sheep moving. I had no watch, but I am sure that it was four o'clock and nearing sundown in that Andean valley, when he caught up with me. He brought a handful of crackers and a quart of whiskey, of which I should say one pint had become an inseparable part of himself. From the moment of his arrival until the tragic time when I herded the sheep into a bend in the creek and began gathering firewood, there was a marked difference in our attitudes toward life and its problems. My companion was optimistic and cheerful to a degree that was almost nauseating, while I who might reasonably be supposed to see the rosy aspect in everything was tossed between rage and apprehension. I felt an immense and unreasonable responsibility for the sheep and I was quite certain that without bedding or adequate clothing I would freeze to death during the night. I could not understand why my employers were not at hand with their promised tent and bedding, to say nothing of provisions, and I feared the worst without knowing what it might be. My comrade was fast asleep when I succeeded in building my fire, and I managed to keep a decent blaze going all through the long night, while I froze on one side and blistered on the other. Next morning we were astir early and on the trail. I was as hungry as any sixteen-year-old boy could be and the herder was aguish and taciturn. After we had traveled about two miles, we got some cold pancakes left over from the family breakfast at a ranch, and these contributed towards filling a long-felt want. For dinner we had spring water, and at sundown after an exhausting day's drive, we reached Laney's at Smith River Canyon. A traveler whom we had met in the afternoon had told us that arrangements had been made for our food and lodging there, but when we reached Laney's, we found that it was some saint's day in Laney's calendar, and while he was perfectly hospitable, he was so drunk that he did little for our comfort except to assure us of his undying esteem. We were by this time desperate men, so we took possession of the cook stove and prepared our own meal, after which we swiped as much clothing and bedding as we could conveniently handle and went down into the meadow where our sheep were folded in a creek bend. I can testify that the herder slept all night, for I hardly closed my eyes.

In the morning I made my first declaration of independence, and the herder, yielding to disquieting signs of rebellion, moved ahead with the sheep, permitting me to rustle breakfast and bring his share to him. In about two hours I had rejoined him, bringing food of a sort, and we trudged on. I was fully determined that there should be an end to this slavery. I had been subjected to treatment not at all in accord with my ideals, and my conception of the relation of labor and capital was becoming quite clearly defined. I contrasted the substantial and appetizing food of my cowboy experience with the husks upon which I was now feeding, and compared the camp life on the trail when a dozen of us were story telling around a cheery campfire, with the exasperating hardships of this employment and the unsatisfactory companionship with my semi-demented fellow sufferer. Although I was nearly forty miles from home, a stranger to the country and its few inhabitants, I had fully determined to "jump the job" when my cheerful and light-hearted employers drove out to meet us from White Sulphur Springs.

Arriving at the little village about sundown, I was given a very satisfactory meal at the hotel and was then invited to go out with one of my employers and sleep with him. The sheep were bunched against a pasture fence and it was supposed that four of us sleeping around the semi-circumference of the drove would keep them quiet for the night, but they were disturbed at intervals by vagrant village dogs, and my night was largely devoted to herding. My companions slept, and as I paced past their comfortably recumbent forms, neither the memory of the substantial supper nor the hope of an appetizing breakfast could shake my determination to sever my connection with the sheep business.

After breakfast upon receiving certain directions from one of my employers, I told him I was going to quit.

"You can't quit," said he.

"I have quit," said I.

"Your mother told us that you would go through to the Judith with us."

"I couldn't live that long," said I.

"We will not pay you unless you go through with us," was the rejoinder.

This was a home thrust. I had spent all the money I had for my new cowboy boots. I was thirty-five miles from home, but I would rather perish on the lonely trail over the mountains than to continue my employment. I was resolved to die game, so I started on foot on the road to the Mussel-shell.

About three miles on the way I crossed a little trout stream and cut a willow stick for a crude alpenstock and washed my tired feet. Commencing my journey anew, I had proceeded hardly half a mile when I was overtaken by the stage coach. The driver, Jamison (blessed be his name), knew me, and asked me what I was doing in that country and on foot? I explained the situation with candor and eloquence and he insisted that I ride. In that country at that time, pedestrian travel was neither safe, sensible, nor common. The moral sense of the community seemed mildly outraged by the spectacle of a man afoot and this feeling was strongly shared by the range cattle. I required little urging to accept the kindly offer. I negotiated my midday meal at Copperopolis on the businesslike basis of deferred payment and reached home that night in a condition approaching normal.

Three days later the band of sheep and its proprietors passed our place. Here again, payment of my wages was refused, and it was necessary to place me under physical and moral bonds to keep the peace. But no battle is lost until it is admitted lost. My father was the lion in the path. He met the itinerants at Judith Gap, and whether it was due to his eloquence (he could speak well when aroused) or because he was a justice of the peace, being recently commissioned, or because he was in the prime of life and weighed two hundred and twenty pounds, the fact remains that my seven dollars and fifty cents was collected, and the two young flock masters went on their way with tingling ears.

My unpleasant experience in this first contact with sheep clinched my determination to be a cowboy. As a step in the right direction, I assisted my father in driving our little herd of cattle to the sawmill, where shelter and hay had been provided for the winter.

When the original herd left Wisconsin, they

were aristocrats all, bearing distinguished, high-sounding names and boasting long pedigrees in the Durham herd book. But the frontier is a great leveler of rank, and our distinguished matrons of the herd were known as, "Limpy," "Loppy," "Milky," and so forth, and this was typical of the treatment accorded human blue blood.

CHAPTER X

TWO WEEKS OF HIBERNATION

ETURNING from this trip, I settled easily and contentedly into my old place as handy man around the trading post and was made conscious of my usefulness when a band of Flathead Indians on their winter visit to the buffalo grounds passed through our settlement. These Indians had been long in contact with the white man, had responded favorably to civilization and differed widely from the Blackfeet I had known at the DHS ranch. They were better armed, better clad, more sophisticated, and devout Catholics to a man. We had little trade with them, for their itinerary had taken them near some of the larger towns to the westward, and they were well equipped. They came, many of them, as old acquaintances, and our little dining room was crowded with invited guests appreciative of my mother's cooking, and the fraternizing was not one sided. We were the recipients of many little gifts and tokens of friendship and sent them away with a cordial and not entirely selfish invitation to pay us a long visit on their return in the spring. Although their visit was short, I discovered three things: that it was beyond my power to acquire even a fragmentary acquaintance with the Flathead language; that the Chinook jargon was necessary and available; and that the universal medium of communication was the sign language.

Thus far we had been favored with ideal fall weather. There now came a young blizzard from the north and with it the "Irish Lord" and his party. This personage who hunted big game in the Rockies for several seasons, was an heir of the Jameson family, distillers. His name has had its prominence on two occasions in Africa. This scion of a wealthy house was an undersized, alert, affable individual who had been crippled in a steeple-chase accident and was hardly able to stand up against the recoil of his heavy rifles. He was a game sportsman, well liked by his guides and hunters. These supernumeraries were discharged at our place and the expedition broke up. The trophies were packed for shipment to Ireland and the three hunters, "Pomp" Dennis, Bob Carpenter, and Sam Elwell, arranged to winter in a comfortable cabin which my father had built in '79 at the head of Mud Creek. They were pretty well provisioned with donations from their former employer and when they invited me to pay them a visit three weeks later, I accepted with great promptness. By this time winter was settled. There was almost no snow on the ground, but the prairie soil and the small streams were hard frozen and there was a consistent chill in the air, ignoring the bright sunshine of our shortened days.

Father's cabin was a cozy log structure with a practical fireplace at one end, a ditto door at the other, and one window, ten by twelve inches, in the east side. My friends had constructed an upper and lower bunk in the corner next the door and improvised four crude stools and a table. The cabin stood in a deep and narrow gulch within twenty feet of a bubbling spring. One corner of the cabin was stacked with provisions, and the pines in the neighborhood were veritable Christmas trees hung with winter meat, elk, black-tail and white-tail deer, antelope, and bighorn. A snow storm setting in about noon the day after my arrival had no terrors for me. We gathered firewood and sat around the cheery fire in our snug cabin with the feeling of satisfaction that every normal individual finds in defying the elements.

While the cold wind howled and the snow sifted from the peaks above us, my hosts, busied about the evening meal, delighted me with stories of their frontier experiences, nor was I sated when a comfortable bed invited me to sleep. Next morning we rolled out when we felt like it—there is no doubt in the world that this is exactly the right time to get up. While the fire was being kindled, I took the water bucket and started for the spring for a supply of fresh drinking water. But I stopped when I opened the door. In front of me was a blank wall of snow. My surprise was extreme but my companions regarded it as quite natural. A considerable quantity of snow had to be shoveled back into the cabin before we could dig out into daylight. We contented ourselves with melted snow for our immediate needs and after breakfast, with some labor, dug a tunnel to the spring. This was considered better than an open cut, which would drift full from day to day. Later we managed to wallow through the snow like amphibians to the steep slope at the east, where the snow was no real impediment to progress and there we amused ourselves by gathering firewood. The floor of the narrow valley was filled to a depth of at least ten feet. The cabin had disappeared, and for more than two weeks, during my entire stay, I never saw its roof. The chimney, projecting perhaps a foot above the snowy surroundings, smoked like a miniature volcano.

It was an era of high living. The choicest cuts of the choicest game were roasted in the coals and our naturally good appetites were stimulated by the imported relishes and condiments donated by Jameson. On warm days our door was left open to give light and air. For me this was a period of pure delight. Two of my companions had served in the Confederate and one in the Northern Army and I was treated to many stories of army experience, invariably humorous. Not all of the stories, however, were warlike.

We had been talking about the telephone, a recent invention none of us had seen, and we recounted the marvels wrought by ingenious Americans. Sam Elwell said that inventiveness might be carried too far. "There was Sol Harkness on Rim Rock Creek. I worked for him one summer getting out poles," said Sam. "He had an attack of ingenuity when he was a kid and it set in. He never did get over it. He had a good sheep ranch where he ought to have made money in sheep, but his soul yearned for better things. He was always tinkering and inventing. The place was full of all sorts of contraptions. There were little whirl-i-gig figures over the cook stove, and toy windmills stuck up on fence posts and everywhere.

"He had a big round table he had built himself, with a merry-go-round contrivance in the middle to put grub on—you didn't have to pass anything. The bill of fare was on the turntable and all you had to do was to turn that thing around to see what your sentence was going to be. It looked pretty clever to me, but one of the fellows told me that they had an awful mix-up in shearing time. They had a big crew and when they were all sitting around the table there was no chance for science, it was infighting from start to finish. I don't know whether it was an overload or not, but the table was inclined to stick, that is the revolver part of it, and one fellow on one side of the table felt a yearning for beans, and another fellow on the other side wanted something else and they began to pull against each other. Finally *one* of them let go and the whole smear went off on a tangent. Everybody took it good-naturedly, he said, except the man who got a bowl of hot gravy in his lap.

"There was a wonderful automatic gate between the ram pasture and the hay corral. It was Harkness's own invention too, and this fellow explained it to me. If you wanted to go in this gate, all you had to do was to drive a little bit haw and hit a great big wooden trigger about two feet high with your nigh wheel. That worked a long lever that tilted a long pole and the gate rolled open on big wooden wheels. When you got through, if you were lucky enough to hit another trigger, that big overhead pole would come down, and the gate would roll shut and latch itself with a big wooden latch.

"There was lots of hard work in that gate. I'll bet it would take a man a month to build one and he would have to be clever too. The main part of the gate was built of lodge-pole pines about six inches apart, and when the gate was shut, the end of each pole plugged right into a hole in the gate post, bored specially for it. The fellow said that the gate had pretty near killed Sol one day when he was down there tinkering with it.

"He had the gate rolled back and was chiseling away at the gate post, when his old milch cow began scratching herself on one of the triggers and turned the gate loose. It whanged shut before Sol got in the clear and caught his head between two of the poles. He was down on his hands and knees with his head sticking through the gate, totally helpless, although he wasn't hurt much. He yelled bloody murder for a while, but he was a long ways from the house and nobody heard him. Then that fool cow came over to investigate. She was gentle and she was inquisitive. First she smelled of Sol's bald head for a while, then she began to lick it. Sol tried to scare her away, but it was no go. I guess human perspiration is salty all right. Finally he got desperate and remembered that she was afraid of the dog, so he commenced barking and growling. Now wouldn't you think that was misery enough for one day? Well, his troubles were just commencing.

"While Sol was bucking and bawling and kicking up his heels, his rams were not paying any attention to him, except one. There was one old devil who had been raised around the house, a kind of pet, and his morals had been corrupted. He was too quarrelsome for any use. He meandered over towards the excitement, and after he had studied the situation for a while (about the time Sol was ready to bite the cow) he turned himself loose and hit the old man so hard that he forgot all about the cow. There is no telling what would have happened if this fellow hadn't come up the creek just then and released the gate.

"While I was there, Sol was working on an improved scarecrow. The coyotes were bothering a good deal and they didn't pay any attention to the old-fashioned scarecrow, but he said that what was needed was something self-moving and that he was the man to invent something. All the time we were building shed, he was at work on his self-propelled scarecrow. He set up two long poles 'bout fifty yards apart along the south side of the garden and strung some wires between them and rigged up a homemade windmill to run the thing. His scarecrow hung from the wires and he had it arranged so that it would go back and forth from one end of its beat to the other. This part of his work wasn't much trouble for him, he said, it was just as easy for him as spitting down a well. The main part of his invention was the scarecrow. He used to talk about it a good deal, and argue. He believed that man was endowed with a superior brain and if an ornery coyote got the best of him, it was because the man didn't really bring his brain into action.

"He made a wonderful dummy with a painted face and a piece of buffalo robe for whiskers; he rigged this thing out with his own clothes, pretty decent clothes too, because he said he wanted it to look like him and he wanted it to smell like him. He had two or three old army overcoats, that was something he always wore in cold weather, and he put one of these on the dummy and tied a wooden gun on its shoulder. It was a wonderful counterfeit all right, and the darned thing worked. The first day that he rigged it up we didn't do much of anything except to watch it. When the wind would freshen, it would go down the swale and up the little rise to the other post, as if the Indians were after it, then whirl around the end and back again, as if it had forgotten something. Sometimes it would stop and think things over and once in a while it would back up for a few feet when an eddy of wind would hit the windmill in the rear, but it worked. I'll say that for it.

"It worked so darned well that Sol lost his ranch. Sol owed some money and needed a lot more (I guess everybody is in the same fix) and he had been trailing along after a sod widow who had just realized on her husband. She was visiting at the MacGregor place down the creek and Sol had just about talked her into lending him three thousand dollars. A day or two after the mechanical sentry was put in operation, the widow drove up from MacGregor's with that quiet old team of his hooked onto a spring wagon. She was nearsighted, but she fetched up alongside of the scarecrow with both horses snorting and she couldn't make them go. She recognized Sol all right, there he was as big as life, whiskers, overcoat, and all, standing still, but not making a move. She spoke to him and asked him to see what was the matter with her horses, but he didn't say a word nor make a move to help her except to sway and nod a little. Just then there came a puff of wind and the dummy rushed at the team, kicked up its heels and started away on the other tack. The widow and the team and the spring wagon held together all right, but they didn't stop until they landed in a patch of bull-berries just across the creek from Mac's place."

· · · · ·

Two Weeks of Hibernation

We played cards and checkers by the light of a spluttering candle of buffalo tallow or looked over back numbers of the *London Illustrated News* by the light from the open door. Here I began my career as a smoker, using a mixture of plug smoking tobacco and the dried leaves of the bear-berry, *l'herbe*, consuming this hot and fragrant blend in an Indian pipe which had once belonged to the famous chief, Red Cloud. We were not in the least interested in the temperature, buried as we were in snow, and when genial weather came indicating the time of my departure, I left camp with sincere regret, carrying with me one of the most pleasant memories of my life.

The widow and the team didn't stop until they landed in the bull berries.

CHAPTER XI

POKER *A LA* MARTINSDALE

EACHING home, I resumed my former rôle at the trading post. This occupation was not arduous, but on occasions when an important poker game was in progress, I might be requested to stay up all night and sometimes had to deal with drunken and dangerous customers. My youth was my greatest protection, and I was compelled on more than one occasion to resort to an acquired guile, learning that what cannot be carried by force may sometimes yield to persuasion. Our scant population was largely made up of young men, foot-loose and with no responsibilities. They were enterprising and alert, quite willing to take a chance. This will explain the popularity of gambling. In our neighborhood there were no exclusive gambling saloons, but poker was very much in evidence, especially in the winter season. It was not unusual for a game to be started in the forenoon; it was very likely to be in full swing during the afternoon, and it was certain to be going full blast throughout the evening, continuing oftentimes on through the night. Gambling was as open and unabashed with us as it is today in the exchanges. The usual poker game was four-handed, and of the four players, one at least was likely to be an itinerant professional, denominated "tin horn." The summer was a busy season and there was less gambling. On most round-ups, card playing was prohibited, not upon the ground of morals, but because it interfered with the work.

I was often called upon to "sit up" with a protracted poker game and ordinarily regarded it a very light duty. At such times I might be called upon to serve an occasional round of drinks or cigars, or to furnish a new deck of cards. I had an opportunity to read and the happy consciousness that no one would scold me for sitting up too late. The gamesters were ordinarily well behaved (men are apt to be civil in a community where everyone is armed), but once in a while bitterness would creep into the game, and my life would be an unhappy one.

One arctic night the steady-going citizens had retired to their blankets, and I was left with four card players for whom life had no sweetness. They were to a man disillusioned and embittered. Every remark was sarcastic or provocative of anger. There was so much ill feeling in the atmosphere that I was pleased to have a diversion, which occurred when our half-grown kitten had an elaborate fit. It yowled and spat, running round in circles, and finally clawed its way up some hanging garments to a high shelf which extended along the wall near the ceiling. There it crouched motionless, but with glaring eyes. Its antics had served to change the conversation, temporarily at least, and the game went on. Before long it was as bad as ever. There was a complicated "jack pot" about to be opened, but whether it was to be opened before the bombardment commenced seemed rather doubtful in my eyes.

I was watching the game very closely to see which player would pick up his revolver first; it was a very tense moment. But again the situation was saved by the kitten, who had another fit. Leaping from his lofty perch, he hurled himself upon that "jack pot" with the utmost fervor. He then made a frantic circuit of the table and flung himself into the bosom of one of the players. Two of the gamblers went over backwards, the other two upset their chairs. Cards, poker chips and two six-shooters went on the floor and the game went into liquidation, very much to my relief.

CHAPTER XII

THE MISSOURIAN

OOKING backward upon Montana as I first saw it, I get the impression of wholesome cleanliness. The streams were sparkling a n d unpolluted, though they might be alkaline. There was no taint in the breezes that strayed to us through the welter of pine-clad mountains; they carried the fragrance of forests, and the winds from the east brought us the scent of sage. The gales swept across Montana as they do today, but they carried no dust. Our frontier was naturally healthful, as might be expected with a population largely composed of robust young men. There was little sickness. Misadventures requiring a surgeon's aid were fraught with tragic possibilities, because the nearest doctor was almost forty miles away.

There were two or three times during our sojourn at the forks of the Musselshell when we were called upon to convert our place into a hospital. I recall one instance and relate it as its memory is filtered through the intervening years. A young fellow was brought in, the ambulance

THE MISSOURIAN

being a lumber wagon in which he was couched
upon a bed of prairie hay. He was too ill to travel
under his own power, but we got him into the ram
pasture and two or three of us who might be called
internes went to work on him. We entered his case
on our records as "male, Missourian, white, twenty-
three years of age." His speech was somewhat in-
coherent, but he told us that he had a misery in his
insides and a right smart fever. Mother took one
look at him and the diagnosis was over and treatment was begun.

We removed his clothes and got him into one of
father's nightshirts. We put his feet to soak in
very hot water, to which had been added a liberal
quantity of mustard. We sponged him off with
cold water and put an ice-pack on his head. It is
my belief that the sack we used for this purpose
had been used for salt, for the pack could not have
been so effective on any other theory. We ad-
ministered a handful of liver pills. (I regret to say
that I do not remember the name on the wooden
box from which the pills were taken, but I presume
that they were those popular and energetic calomel
pills so dear to our ancestors.) About this time
mother came in with two quarts of strong sage
tea, brewed from the wild sage so plentiful in our
locality. I do not know that this decoction was
strong enough to float a kingbolt, but it was very

potent, and the patient drank until he was all awash and we could hear a faint sizzling in his ears. His feet were pretty well parboiled by this time, his head was completely refrigerated, and whatever may have been his opinion of our treatment, a great step had been taken in psychotherapy; the patient knew absolutely that "pain is error," and he must have had a surmise that he was under treatment.

We got him into a bunk, removed the polar cap and began the real medication, a substantial foundation having been laid for the *real* curative agent. Mother dropped three or four pellets of a homeopathic specific into a glass of water and the patient was required to take one teaspoonful every fifteen minutes. Whether the pellets were *nux vomica* or *arsenicum album*, I know not, perhaps it does not matter, but I do know that in two or three days his disease had been routed, and in three or four more he had so far recovered from our treatment that he could get his boots on. We never knew the cause of his illness, but mother's theory was that he had been doing his own cooking.

CHAPTER XIII

THANKSGIVING

HE Thanksgiving season has a twofold character; there must be the spirit of t h a n k f u l n e s s, of course, but there must also be present the symbols of the occasion. We had many reasons for thankfulness: meat was plentiful; the potato harvest had been a bountiful one; there had been no Indian hostilities; livestock was in good condition and the country was settling up with a good class of neighbors. Herds of cattle and bands of sheep were being driven eastward into the Musselshell, the Judith Basin, and the neighborhood of Fort Maginnis, which had just been established. We could look forward to the winter with equanimity, especially as we had no foreknowledge of its character. We had the spirit of Thanksgiving, but the symbols were absent. We could remember roast turkey, celery, cranberries, raw oysters, and squash pie, as parts of a delectable menu quite unobtainable in the wilds of Montana.

In planning our Thanksgiving dinner we could command, it is true, some very good substitutes for the conventional viands. There was, for instance, roast buffalo hump. Please remember that *our* buffalo meat was taken from fat young cows, and was not part of the carcass of undesirable bulls culled from preserved herds. We had also elk, deer, and antelope hams to select from. We had pickled beaver tail and jams and jellies from the chokecherry and buffalo-berry, but all of these seemed to lack authority. From the consideration of delicacies quite beyond our reach, we began to consider foods more staple in their nature, but equally hard to obtain. For instance, there was a general hankering for fresh pork sausage, but there were no pigs in our section of the country and we might as well have wished for fresh lobster. So long did we consider this toothsome and appetizing meat product that at last, in sheer desperation, we ventured upon a substitute.

We had in store some large fat sides of dry salted pork. Some of this meat combined with elk meat was chopped and seasoned, and the creators pronounced it good! Now if we had some cider, but cider was not to be had and it is quite certain that there were no apples nearer than White Sulphur Springs. One box of this fruit had come into the settlement in October and it had come in style on a stagecoach all the way from Utah. Each individual apple, small and unassuming as it was, had sold for two bits. Our success with the synthetic sausage induced us to take one more step in the downward path of substitution. The standard and in fact almost the only dried fruit obtainable was the old-fashioned dried apple—apples really dried, not evaporated. The quartered fruit in this ancient drying process was strung like beads upon strings and dried in the sun. The finished fruit had the rich color of an old saddle. We took a large quantity of this mistreated fruit and put it to soak; when thoroughly soaked, it was worked through a sieve and strained through a cloth. The resulting liquor seemed to lack "bouquet"; we added a little vinegar; that made the tipple too sour; we added sugar until the sourness was overcome, and then, as a finishing touch, we carelessly added a cupful of whiskey.

At our Thanksgiving dinner the sausage was declared by men who had not tasted pork sausage for years to be unexcelled; the cider was praised in equally high terms and the squash pie, made of carrots, was also awarded special honors.

That Thanksgiving was a proud and memorable day for all of us who participated in the preparation of the dinner. The dining room itself, which was also the kitchen, seemed filled and permeated with the spirit of the occasion, and well it might be, for it had the proud distinction of being the only cabin in the place with a board floor. The long table was covered with a turkey-red table-cloth and adorned with an elaborate silver service, relics of former greatness, and the whole place was illuminated, not by home-made buffalo-fat candles, but by two kerosene lamps.

It is quite probable that thirty people were fed at our dinner, in relays, of course. The first who came were seated on the long bench next the wall, others were given individual stools of home manufacture. Within those rough-hewn walls and under that dirt roof there was something not material; there was youth, health, and strength; there was optimism and courage; a spirit of friendliness and comradeship; and these things may have been absent from other more formal and pretentious observances of the day.

This Thanksgiving dinner is the only one I can remember when we did not have at least a few of the viands appropriate to the occasion. By the following year we could obtain turkey, cranberries, celery, and canned raw oysters.

I am quite sure that following our Thanksgiving feast we gave the first grand ball ever held in the Musselshell Valley. There were five women present, including our half-breed girl, who jigged through the measures of the square dances in calico and moccasins.

To the male dancers we sold fifty tickets which were numbered serially. Numbers one to four were first called, the holders being privileged to dance if they could obtain partners for the set. Others were called in their order and there was some bartering for preferred positions in the schedule. The fiddler and his music grew very mellow as the hours advanced, but a "pleasant time was enjoyed by all."

CHAPTER XIV

A BLIZZARD, A MURDER, AND A FIGHT

HERE was little travel that winter and trade was dull. The range cattle received no attention, and the flocks of sheep were kept at the home ranches. I discovered that winter in Montana was different in most respects from the same season in Wisconsin. This was the historic hard winter of '80 and '81, and I was to experience for the first time a truly terrible blizzard. This storm in its ordinary manifestations is an outburst of northern fury lasting about three days, but this winter the storm continued for fully two weeks, and range stock perished, not so much from starvation as from absolute freezing.

After the storm had continued beyond reasonable bounds and was still raging, an exodus of cattle from the upper valleys set in and for two or three days there filed past our place along the river bottom a discouraged and hopeless procession of cattle, hungry and freezing, driven by their distress. It was bitterly cold, with a strong gale

blowing from the north, truly perishing weather.
I could compare the flight to nothing but pictures
I had seen of the retreat from Moscow. We were
two weeks without mail or any communication
with the outside world, but suffered no personal
inconvenience or hardship. Our mud-topped
cabins were warm, our larder was well stocked,
and for us this blizzard, which spelled disaster for
some, was only tiresome. As all things must end,
so this storm ended, and my memory of the winter
is that its strength was spent in this abnormal
outburst.

We took advantage of open weather, long before
the advent of spring, to send teams to Judith Gap
to bring in a considerable stock of merchandise
which had been left where the freighter, traveling
from Fort Benton to our place, had encountered the
first fall storm, when I was enjoying the hospitality
of the hunter's cabin. Our bull-whacker had lost
his cattle—they had drifted before the heavy
storm—and did not recover them until the next
summer. Our goods, protected only by the wagon
boxes and canvas coverings, remained at the point
where he had been deprived of his motive power.
Our bottled beer was not only a total loss, but
being on top of cases of clothing, had damaged a
great deal of stock that would ordinarily have been
unaffected by freezing and thawing. We re-

plenished our supplies of flour, sugar, tobacco, and cartridges without loss, and went into the spring pretty well stocked—a little short of beer, but with plenty of whiskey.

With the coming of spring weather there was an opportunity for a boy to earn money by skinning cattle that had perished during the winter and I undertook the unpleasant task with an enthusiasm that waned perceptibly. I spent several cold and comfortless days at this most disagreeable occupation and sold my spoils for thirty-five dollars, with which I purchased my first cowboy saddle.

And now before settled spring weather, with the hills barely showing green through the grass, our Flathead friends visited us on their return to their homes west of the divide. Their coming was like the advent of the circus, a few scouts in advance, followed by a long procession of riders, ponies with lodge-poles or travois packed with the winter's spoils, the whole cavalcade wearing a general air of prosperity and well being. Near the tail of the procession came quite a herd of loose horses, many bearing packs. I remember one cantankerous mare that carried an Indian pack saddle with a light load. On one side in a rawhide pouch there were three well-trained pups, on the other side an equally well-trained papoose. The old mare was loose and seemed to think that her purpose in life was to discipline the other horses, for she ran from one to another, biting or kicking as the case seemed to require, but her cargo was never disturbed.

We had a lively trade for two days or so, and I had an occasion to air my knowledge of the Chinook and sign language which I had picked up during the winter months. We invited one Indian to come behind the counter as interpreter and house detective. This individual was at once conscious of his elevated and important station, and helped himself to stick candy, dried apples and crackers, until I was sure he would die, but he lived through it and was really of great service to us. A few of our Indian friends were again invited to sit at mother's table, where they behaved with more real gentility than many of our Caucasian guests. Their visit was profitable and would have been wholly pleasant, if unscrupulous whites had not furnished them with liquor.

With the party were two Pend d'Oreille Indians who had been with the Flatheads during the winter hunt. To relieve the tedium of buffalo hunting they had gone on a successful horse stealing expedition into the Crow country on the Yellowstone. But the Flatheads, mindful of the adage that a man is known by the company he keeps, would not permit the stolen horses to be taken west, but left them with us upon our promise that the Crow agent should be notified and the horses returned. After the main party had left our place, the two Pend d'Oreilles came back, drunken and defiant, and took their booty from the corral. They had hardly proceeded a quarter of a mile before they were met and halted by young Charlo, son of the chief.

We were distant witnesses of the altercation which ended in the killing of the young chief and the flight of the suddenly sobered murderers. In the greatest possible haste they left their victim and rode to the protecting timber along the south fork of the Musselshell, emerging shortly after upon the hill south of the stream. A loyal Flathead Indian, delayed at our place, made a hurried demand for a "big gun." He was given a '76 Winchester and a handful of ammunition. The distance was about eight hundred yards and there were no obstructions. We could see the spiteful little spurts of dust where the bullets struck the dry hillside, just under, just over, just behind the targets, but the fleeing Indians lashed their horses into a frantic burst of speed while they resorted to the Indian style of making their horses' bodies protect their own. They were soon out of sight as well as out of range, and the young chief was buried unavenged.

A Blizzard, a Murder, and a Fight

I had another glimpse of the savage side of the frontier before our reluctant spring was really at hand. In this case the savagery was displayed by the white man. Among the denizens of our little community, there was a long-haired individual known as "Yellowstone," an unsafe, erratic man, a boaster and a blowhard, of doubtful metal and unstable composition, a man who might be dangerous. There was also Matt Shirley, a lean Texas cowboy past the first flush of youth, but with the freckles and devil-may-care attributes of that period of life, hardened mentally and physically by years of frontier experience. These gentlemen, meeting at an informal evening entertainment at the camp of "Whiskey Meyers," chanced to differ on some question under discussion, and "Yellowstone" left the party, taking first to the water and then to the brush, shortly ahead of a salute of two guns.

Shirley was convinced of two things, first that his gunpowder had not been burned in vain, and that "Yellowstone's" bullet-pierced body was floating down the Musselshell and second, that he had shot in self-defense. In order to fortify his position he came to our peaceful abode with a demand for my father, who, as justice of the peace, represented the majesty of the law. Shirley seemed quite unhappy when he was informed that my father was absent and that none of us were willing to accept his surrender.

On the morning after this occurrence it chanced that I was sent on an errand to the cabin where Shirley lodged. On my way I met "Yellowstone" carrying a rifle over his arm and he informed me he was looking for Shirley. When I reached Shirley's cabin, with the benevolent idea that Shirley might wish to make his escape, I told him that "Yellowstone" was hunting for him. Shirley replied with a grin that there was nobody easier to find. He buckled on his six-shooter belt and walked briskly to Clendennin's cabin whither "Yellowstone" had preceded him. I followed, scenting battle. Peering cautiously from behind a protecting door-jamb, I watched the development of the affair. "Yellowstone" had the approved position for defense, but not for retreat, seated in a corner of the room with his long rifle standing at his right hand. Shirley walked in blithely and across the room, where, after twining his fingers in the unresisting "Yellowstone's long hair, he proceeded to beat him about the head with his Colt's six-shooter. It is to be supposed that the blows were somewhat tempered, for no fatality resulted. We had, instead, the spectacle of a gory and chastened man, who soon left the settlement.

Chapter XV

I AM DAY HERD

I HAD now spent a year in Montana, a period of impressions, adjustments, and valuations. I had opened the great book of the frontier, but was still absorbed in the pictures without finding time for the reading of the text. My employment at the trading post was desultory and to me quite unsatisfactory. I had seen enough of the seamy side of whiskey-selling to have a horror of it, and my hope and ambition was to get real employment and help provide for the family. Father's sawmill was in operation, its success hampered by an over-taxed and leaky boiler. Mother's dining room was crowded and profitable, but she was overworked and unable to get help. My happiness may be imagined when I was hired as day herder for the horses of the Musselshell round-up at thirty-five dollars per month "and found."

There were a few days of mild and good-natured rioting during the gathering of the clans before the work of the spring commenced. The puncheon floor of our emporium was riddled with bullets and a considerable quantity of our precious kerosene was wasted upon the floor of our cellar. Nothing to be seriously condemned—boys will be boys—and all damage was paid for either in cash or readily accepted promises.

It has been said that every successful man is, at some time, a heavy borrower, and this was my borrowing period. Beyond my saddle I had almost nothing in the way of equipment. I managed to assemble a reasonably complete outfit, excepting *chaparejos,* the lack of which gave me much occasion for lament.

I was now fairly launched upon a career of my choosing and I feel certain that most boys of seventeen would be willing to exchange with me. The round-up at that time numbered about fifty men, a somewhat nondescript aggregation, as compared to the larger round-ups when the range industry had attained its height. The dominant majority of the cowboys were Texas men, bred to the business and bringing with them the code and traditions of the cow-camp. But we had a number of glorified farm hands, young men from the old ranches in western Montana, as familiar with the plow as they were with the lasso, and there were a few, like myself, who escaped the derisive appellations, "pilgrim" and "tenderfoot" by a very narrow margin. In spite of superficial diversities, the round-up was homogeneous in one significant aspect—the riders were young. Two or three graybeards, mounted upon placid ponies, took their part in riding circle and came in, industrious and dusty, at the rear of the herd, but the presence of these patriarchs (men approaching fifty) was pure emphasis upon the dominant note—youth. We are prone to think of the men of earlier generations as bent and grizzled veterans. I can testify that the men who fought in our Civil War were mere youths. The testimony of forty-niners I have known is conclusive to the fact that the pioneers of California were boys or very young men and not the gray antiques generally depicted. It may be said in a general way that our group was composed of boys, youths, and young men, many of them old in experience, serving almost from childhood in the cow-camps of the Southwest, hardened and tempered by life on the lawless frontier.

The horses of the round-up, some three hundred in number, were to be guarded and handled during the day by another youth and myself. My co-worker was a boy of my own age, Montana born, and much my superior in wisdom and efficiency. Our comradeship was somewhat imperfect on this account, but we managed to get along together fairly well throughout the long season.

The range cattle in the Musselshell Valley carried brands of some fifteen or twenty different owners, who united in the work of rounding-up, branding, and gathering for shipment, and the work was done under the direction of a captain selected by them. My comrade and I were the servants of this association and in common with the other riders were under the captain's orders. After a few days our work was so much a matter of routine that no instructions were needed. We received the loose horses as soon as the team horses and mounts for the morning's work had been caught. When the mess wagons were on their way to the new camp and the riders were making their circle, we drifted our herd over the intervening miles to the scene of the midday operations, where the demand for fresh mounts was varied by circumstances. If the round-up chanced to be complete at an early hour, two or three riders would be left to hold the tired cattle, while the others took their noonday meal, after which new horses would be caught for all. On other occasions the work of cutting out and branding would be in progress before the arrival of all the riders from distant parts of the circle, and we were compelled to be at hand so that late comers could replace their tired mounts and take part in the afternoon's work. The released horses would come nickering to the herd all through the afternoon, and it was only necessary for us to bring in the herd in the evening, so that the night herders might get their horses and end our day of sixteen hours or thereabouts. The work was not arduous. After a few days there was no tendency toward straying, the herd instinct was strengthened, and our band of horses were so homogeneous that our work was rendered very simple.

There was the usual variety of weather in the spring and early summer. The scene of our operations was changing from day to day as we moved into new territory and built new corrals to work portions of the range which heretofore had known only the buffalo and the Indian. It was hardly a week after we started that I suffered a humiliation which was peculiarly devastating, because I was so anxious to appear well in the eyes of my new associates. I think we were in camp near the mouth of Big Elk Creek. It had rained rather heavily during the night, the tent had blown down and I had slept very little. We took our herd out in the rain, but by ten o'clock the sky cleared and the country was steaming like an Indian's sweat-lodge. I was desperately sleepy, but the ground was too wet and muddy to think of dismounting for a nap. At this juncture I had a brilliant inspiration. I was riding a Texas saddle, a Fort Sill tree, with a horn about the size of a pie plate and a very low cantle. I reversed my position in the saddle, with my feet in front of the stirrups. I pillowed my head on my folded arms on the horse's rump and in almost no time at all I was sleeping blissfully.

How long my nap continued I do not know, but when I waked, the horse herd was running and my horse was galloping in the rear. I did not fall off. I did not lose my stirrups, but the ride was not enjoyable. I tried to get the reins, but they were clear down next to the horse's ears, and I couldn't reach them; besides, I had my work cut out for me to keep on top, without trying to change ends. The herd ran around the camp once or twice, my horse jumping a ditch which nearly ruined me, and finally my partner stopped the horse fairly in the center of our camp.

Then I tried to dismount in the ordinary way, but my spur caught in the horse's mane, just enough to make the effort rather comic. As I stood with one foot on the ground on the wrong side of the horse, he stepped forward smartly, which was backward from my point of view. My foot stuck in the stirrup for an instant, and I dug my face in the mud. Then I got up and stepped in my hat, and my spur caught in the sweatband and tore it loose. My misadventure was complete, and the worst of it was that I had a large and appreciative audience. If there is any pain more poignant than the embarrassment of an adolescent, I have been spared the experience.

He nearly ruined me when he jumped the ditch.

CHAPTER XVI

THE RAWHIDE LASSO

I WAS almost surfeited with novelty. The work itself, the wild animals, the untracked prairie, the traditions, manners, and standards were all new to me. In company with these frontiersmen I was the veriest tyro. It was necessary for me to learn from the humblest beginnings to catch, saddle, ride my horse, and how to use the lasso, and I found that the technic of these arts was much more involved than I had supposed. In everything that I wished to learn I found antagonistic and competing schools, and I regret to say that in more than one instance I followed the wrong leadership. I was at least industriously imitative and became fairly expert with the lasso in the course of a few months.

My grandchildren will read of the lasso and its use in their stories of the frontier, just as they will read of the bolas in tales of the pampas, but it is not likely that they will ever see one in use. The standard rope was of braided rawhide, fifty feet in length, with a diameter of seven-sixteenths of an inch. It was the product of home industry.

UBET

A selected part of the hide of a two-year-old beef was soaked for a few days in water to which wood ashes had been added. Then four long strips, half an inch wide were cut, and stretched under equal tension to dry. When dry, the hair was scraped off with a sharp knife, and the stretched strands, now of uneven width, were trimmed uniformly. The strands were now rolled up and soaked again for another stretching, after which they were again trimmed for uniformity. This was followed by a careful trimming of the corners, and the finished strand with its pointed oval section was perhaps three-eighths of an inch wide and one-sixteenth of an inch thick. The four strands, moistened for flexibility, were easily braided into a single rope, approximately round and of the desired length. In its rope form, following another soaking and stretching, it was trimmed where necessary with a sharp knife and sandpapered for smoothness, after which is was thoroughly greased with beef suet and reduced to reasonable flexibility by drawing it through holes bored in a post or log. The loop end was provided with a rawhide "honda" or eye and the strands at the other end were secured so that they would not unbraid. The finished product was a rope, strong, not too limber, heavy in proportion to its bulk, and, best of all, maintaining those quali-ties so that the adept was not compelled to change his technique from day to day, as was the case if he relied upon a manila or sisal rope. The only objection to the rawhide lasso was its temperamental susceptibility to moisture. It could not be used in rainy weather.

With this simple instrument, the adept cowboy performed, in the course of his daily work, some very remarkable feats, having some of the characteristics of legerdemain. To catch a running animal by the selected foot was commonplace; to throw a loop over the horns or to catch by the neck was even more simple; and to throw the "figure eight," catching the fleeing animal by the neck and both front feet in a twisted loop was not impossible. The loop, swung in a circle over the head, was thrown with a motion not unlike the one used in throwing a ball, but to *throw* the lasso was not enough; the reserve rope held tightly coiled in the left hand must be paid out with great judgment, and the flying loop as it reached its destination must be checked and closed by the right hand, which an instant before had hurled it. Then at the exact moment the tightening rope was given a turn or two around the horn of the saddle, the horse was checked and controlled, the rider shifted his weight to ease the shock and assist his horse in holding the captured animal. Altogether, so much co-ordination was required between the trained muscles and mind of both rider and horse, that the description of even the simplest roping is almost impossible.

One day we moved camp from American Forks to Fish Creek. Arrived at the camp site, I rode to the top of a hill and watched the contented horses bury their sensitive noses in the delicious grass of the valley, enjoying their first uninterrupted feast of the day. The mess wagons took up their selected positions near the stunted willows of the stream, the draught horses were unharnessed and turned loose, and the cooks began rustling wood. The outlook for fuel was not promising, even green willows, execrable fuel, were scarce, but there was a chance that driftwood might be found among the greasewood on the bottom land. I saw the cooks searching through the knee-high scrubby growth of the alluvial valley and, noting their lack of success, I allowed my eyes to assist in the search. Not far from where they were loosely grouped I saw in the shade of a blighted willow a desirable piece of drift, and with natural loyalty, I shouted the information to the cook of our mess. He started for the prize with commendable promptness, followed by four or five others, and I saw a hot foot-race, with considerable shouting and skylarking. Then, very much to my astonishment, when they had nearly reached their goal, they stopped with remarkable unanimity and raced back to the wagons, coming back more sedately with their rifles. It can be imagined that I was considerably mystified by this behavior and somewhat astonished when, after the first shot, the drift log leaped into the air and did not resume its loglike character until quite a volley had been fired. Dinner was perhaps a little late, but we had the skin of a mountain lion to explain the delay.

At the easternmost limit of our range, near Careless Creek, we picked up twelve or fourteen stray horses bearing a western Montana brand. They had evidently escaped from horse thieves who were driving them to the horse thief headquarters on the Missouri. I was to learn more about horse thief activities in years to come.

The spring round-up being completed, I accepted with much pleasure the wages for my work and with greater pleasure the promise that I could have the same place in the fall round-up. My liabilities were liquidated and I enjoyed a vacation at home, a solvent member of the settlement.

When the work of branding fall calves and gathering beef began, I took up my old position with my comrades of the spring round-up and went through the autumn work very much as a matter of course. There were two experiences on the fall round-up that perhaps are worthy of record, and one, my close approach to disgrace, shall be first told.

CHAPTER XVII

A HORSE RACE AND A STAMPEDE

O NE OF the cattle owners was the complacent possessor of a once famous race horse, known throughout Montana as "Caribou," a veteran six-hundred-yard horse. "Chet" Bostwick, a reckless young cow puncher, had in his string a sorrel colt showing symptoms of speed, and it seemed that some discussion had arisen concerning the speed merits of the two horses.

One day when we had made no change of camp, waiting the completion of a corral, I was herding alone at some distance from camp, my side partner laying off on account of some minor injury. To me there came in the most casual and innocent way, Bostwick, on the Two Dot sorrel. After an interchange of innocuous repartee, it was suggested as a happy thought that we try the sorrel and Caribou. This was accordingly done in a thorough manner and I was surprised to find that Caribou was much slower than his reputation. I was considerably disquieted when Bostwick told me that our experience was to remain a profound secret and that if I whispered a word of what had occurred, I should do so under penalty of death. I was more disquieted when I found upon return to camp in the evening that a match race had been arranged between the horses and that long odds were being offered on the decrepit Caribou. The matter was really serious, and my perturbation not without occasion. What might have been the outcome I cannot say, but I was eventually relieved of my embarrassment when I found that the secret had leaked out and was known to everyone in camp. Bostwick, anxious to make as big a killing as possible, had taken in a few friends with the usual result. The captain of the round-up declared all bets off and the race was run for pure joy. My only punishment was a sobering lecture from the captain and a vast amount of well-deserved chaff.

The other outstanding experience was the night stampede of four thousand beef cattle. It is hard to justify any attempt to handle so many beef steers in one herd, but we were short-handed, and the cattle had been gathered very rapidly. It was planned to divide the herd on the next day, but before the coming of day the stampede had occurred. The night threatened storm. The herd, from its size, to say nothing of the natural wildness of the cattle, had been very hard to handle during the day, and at nightfall, which came with gusts of wind and pelting showers of rain, twenty-five riders were given the task of holding the herd through the night. Our camp was in the river valley and the herd was bedded in the low bench-land to the north. Before we were asleep, the herd had stampeded across the river below camp, and be-tween that time and midnight it seemed that no more than an hour passed without its stampede. They ran from one side of the river to the other, below us, above us. The earth trembled and the air reverberated with their bellowings and the sound of clashing horns. I had no confidence in twelve-ounce duck as protection against the mad-dened horde, and yet I was ashamed to move my bed to the wagon. I can truly say that my sleep, even after midnight, was broken.

The fall round-up finished, I invested some of my wages in a new Montana-made saddle, after disposing of my first one. My new saddle was a cumbrous, double-cinch agglomeration of leather and saddler's hardware, for which I paid fifty hard dollars, and I rode it to our new home in Judith Gap, which was in process of construction. The location finally decided upon was about half a mile down the valley from the original claim cabin which my father had put up in '79. The place was an open, grassy, intermountain valley, the

Belt Mountains being two miles to the southwest and the Snowy Range twelve miles to the eastward. In the meadow to the south of the location, there was a large spring of good water. It was located in the Judith Gap where the popular Fort Benton road joined the old Carroll Trail.

CHAPTER XVIII

UBET

THE NEW home was well planned and eventually well built. The first building constructed was the ice-house, and in rapid succession the barn, the saloon, and the hotel were put up. The hotel building was about thirty-six by forty-eight, two stories in height, built and ceiled with sawed and planed lumber from father's sawmill, and for the times was a remarkably fine structure. While the hotel was being completed, we sheltered ourselves where we might, in the ice-house, saloon, or barn, and while in this posture, we experienced our only Indian scare.

One bright day, while everyone was busy, someone not too busy to look up saw a group of scattered horsemen on a hill about two miles distant. Inspection with the field glass showed that they were Indians in full regalia. There was instant alarm. Every man found his rifle and ammunition; two tubs of water were carried into the saloon building for use in case of a siege, and plans were made for the best defense possible, when the observer with the field glass, very much to our relief, announced that the Indians had been followed by a detachment of soldiers. In a few minutes we were hobnobbing with Cheyenne scouts, the innocent cause of our panic, and giving salute to the passing troops.

For several years there had been no serious Indian trouble in our locality, but the menace was present. Even the children sensed the possibility of danger. One spring day my ten-year-old sister and eight-year-old brother were permitted to go hunting to Ross's Fork, two or three miles away, in the fond hope of killing a duck. Armed with a small shotgun and one cartridge, mounted double upon a slow and safe cayuse pony, they soon reached the border of willows along the stream. While they were searching for ducks, they saw at some distance down the valley a body of horsemen rapidly approaching. Concluding that they were in the path of a war party, they hurriedly consulted upon preparations for defense. Deciding that their horse was too slow to enable them to escape mounted, they removed their shoes and stockings so that they could run faster and took up a strong defensive position under the steep bank of the stream. To make their weapon more terribly dangerous, they carefully filled the barrel to its muzzle with fine selected gravel, and awaited the attack. The horsemen proved to be detached cowboys in playful pursuit of a buffalo, and thus a terrible slaughter was averted.

It was during this winter that I rode my first bucking horse, for a moment or two. I had acquired in some manner a stylish little mare who was known as a bucker. I had never ridden her and more especially I had never ridden a bucking horse, but I was quite accustomed to the saddle. I had seen many bucking horses and I was equipped with the necessary paraphernalia. When in costume, I very much resembled a *vaquero*. We had with us at that time a family of Minnesota pilgrims, and they were desirous of seeing a display of western horsemanship, so I, as the only representative of the cowboy element, volunteered to give an exhibition. I still marvel at my foolhardiness. The idea that I might be thrown never entered into my calculations. If I reasoned at all upon the subject I must have convinced myself that, having all the necessary properties, the part could not be hard to play. With perfect equanimity I saddled the little mare, watched her pitch around the corral in a vain endeavor to be rid of the saddle, and then with a cigarette negligently drooping from one corner of my mouth and with my tenderfoot audience clinging to the corral fence like so many pieces of washing, I mounted with faultless technic. If I could at this point draw a veil over the disaster, it would have to be done very quickly. I am told that it was the fourth jump that found me quite separate and distinct from my mount. Fortunately I landed in a soft place, and when I had cleaned the soft place from my clothes, I was little the worse for the encounter.

There was little travel during the winter, but with the arrival of spring and the completion of our necessary buildings, a tide of immigration set in. The roads were thronged with home seekers, and those already located were returning for their families and their flocks and herds. Our new establishment needed post office facilities and a name. During a visit in Helena, my father made application to Major Martin Maginnis, our territorial delegate, who had been an officer in my father's regiment during the Civil War. The assurance that the post office would be established was promptly given and upon being asked for a name, father made the impromptu reply, "Ubet." The name had the advantage of being unique and short; it had the disadvantage of being undignified, but it served.

CHAPTER XIX

COW PUNCHING IN EARNEST

EARLY in May 1882, I left home and went into the employ of the DHS outfit, attached to a small party going into the Musselshell to receive a bunch of cattle bought on the range. There were about twelve men in our outfit, of whom only two or three had served with the company in 1880. One of these was a unique character, "Roach" Chapman, a young "web-foot" who had come through from Oregon with one of the DHS herds. He was an able cowman and a good rider, but his distinguishing characteristic was his dare-deviltry. He was utterly lawless, a happy-go-lucky, unreliable friend, and an enemy to be feared. No small boy carried a chip more constantly on his shoulder than did Roach Chapman, the boss of our outfit.

The cattle business had grown faster than the population. Men were scarce, but horses were scarcer, and I received extra pay in consideration of furnishing two horses. One was the little mare that had brought down the towering edifice of my conceit and the other was an industrious old plodder named Morgan. Morgan shall be remembered not for his virtues but for his vices. No horse could fall down oftener than he, and had he been as swift as he was inept a private cemetery would have been necessary for his riders. As it was, the falls I suffered from his stumblings were only semi-tragic. The real tragedy was the fact that I could not complain of my own horse. If he had been a company horse, I could have refused to accept him. One evening it was discovered that my little mare was missing from the herd. She was always an aloof spirit. Next day, while I was slumbering among the willows in a mosquito-infested valley, she was returned to the herd in a characteristic Roach Chapman fashion. A cowboy employed by one of the big Musselshell outfits had noticed the little mare grazing alone not far from the '79 camp. He ran her into the company bunch and, not finding anyone who knew her brand, took possession of her as a stray. Next day he saddled and rode her with considerable pleasure, until he met the redoubtable Roach. This was in the days when every man was armed, but I sing of "Arms and the Man." With no display of belligerency except some perfect teeth revealed in an equivocal smile, Roach made the other rider dismount and unsaddle. Under his compelling eye the expostulating misdemeanant shouldered his saddle and outfit and was driven into his camp under the lashing of a heavy quirt, effectively applied. It was a dare-devil thing to do. There was a clan spirit in every outfit, and the spectacle was a humiliation to every member of the '79 mess.

Our sole business on the Musselshell range was to receive and hold the newly purchased cattle. We were not concerned in the regular rounding up and branding. From the beginning, when our herd was small enough to be corralled at night, it was only a few days until the corrals could no longer hold them and we commenced night herding. I was selected as one of the two night herders. This was my first experience at night work. At first my distaste for this feature of cowboy life was so pronounced that I could willingly have given up my cowboy career. My condemnation of it had no qualifications. The nights were periods of cold, wet, and wholly miserable penance, fit for sins I had never committed. I was poorly mounted and, worst of all, inexperienced. The hours of seemingly impenetrable darkness were never ending. My companion was surly and unsociable and my defense was inadequate against his boorishness. My first retaliatory attempt was noticeably unsuccessful.

After a night during which hardly one civil word had been exchanged, we were relieved and sat on opposite sides of a camp fire warming our chilled fingers and toes. The cook was busy at his proper fire and we were enjoying the warmth of the embers of a real he fire which the boys had built the evening before. As we sat there, my nose detected the odor of burning cloth. I had already warned my companion that he might be sitting too near the embers, but he had resented my well-meant warning, so I remained silent while the fumes increased. I even took some pleasure in conjecturing the velocity and direction of his leap when he should discover himself on fire. Revenge is an unworthy passion, and to find happiness in the discomfort of others is unmanly. It was my *own* coat tail that was on fire, and, after I had extinguished the conflagration, my only consolation was in the fact that some minor alterations might convert the ruin of the long-tailed "sourdough" overcoat into a more convenient reefer. The nights were getting warmer anyway.

The cattle who tenanted the foothills and the prairies so recently vacated by the buffalo were somewhat nondescript in character, of diverse origins and not at all uniform in physical characteristics, as were the Spanish cattle of the South. They were of good size, red, white, and roan, with some brindles and a few blacks and duns. According to modern standards their horns were too large and long for any popular breed, although to distinguish them from the Longhorns of Texas, they were called Shorthorns. This name was applied with no great impropriety, for they were, in reality, grade Durhams. Their ancestors had followed the trail behind prairie schooners of the Mormon or Oregon settlers, or that great migration to California after the gold discovery. The pioneers in western Montana found their little herds grown to unmanageable proportions, and gradually the increase in native stock filled the valleys east of the Rockies, one by one. Large herds trailed through the welter of mountains from Utah, Oregon, and Washington to new pastures in the buffalo land, and at the time of the decline of the range cattle industry, some herds were driven up from Texas into our country. The descendants of Blossom and Sukey, the family milch cows, reverted to a feral state in their new freedom, where they fought for their lives against the wolves and coyotes, and saw their enemy, man, but twice a year. Timidity was their characteristic, changed to reckless ferocity when they were much harried.

The real and vital accomplishment of the cowboy was the completeness of his knowledge of bovine psychology. He studied their moods and habits, he watched their movements for indications of their mental states, he listened in the dark for sounds expressive of herd opinion, and in the form of song he made his plea for conservatism during the long night. It must never be thought that the cow has a good ear for music. If this were true, the herd would have been stampeded by his songs. The cowboy sang at night in order that the animals might be conscious always of his presence and to avoid startling them by unannounced approach. Talking was as effective as singing, but no sane man will talk to himself for hours at a stretch.

In course of time I found myself. The depressing difficulties of my position were found to be largely imaginary, the majority of our ever-growing herd was becoming trail broke, and we were coming into the season of short nights, when night herding can be really pleasant.

CHAPTER XX

TRIALS OF THE TRAIL

WHEN we finished gathering the purchased herd, we were ready for our drive to the home ranch, only a hundred miles away. But this part of the summer's work, so simply stated, was the most heart-breaking bit of cow punching I ever experienced. We encountered nearly two weeks of belated rain. It is bad enough to stay in camp for a fortnight in such weather, but to make and break camp every day is worse than bad. Every night our tents were pitched in wet grass and our sodden bedding spread to absorb more moisture. Every morning the saturated total of our equipment was bundled into its imperfect shelter in the wet mess wagon. We were short handed, and night herded half the night. Four hours of sleep out of the twenty-four is hardly sufficient. We were completely water-logged, with our decks washed by every sea, when the deluge ceased and the sun came out with its old-time fervor. This occurred when we were driving our herd up a narrow mountain valley, which in a moment became as full of warm vapor as a laundry. This was the time when I fell asleep in the saddle and tumbled to the ground, and the first occasion when I rubbed tobacco juice in my eyes to keep them open. We reached the home ranch the next day, and were given two weeks of absolute idleness to recompense us for our overwork on the trail.

In that time of leisure and recreation I made myself quite at home at the DHS ranch, which I had first seen two years before. I visited Fort Maginnis, now a fully built and established frontier military post, and the mining camp, Maiden, about six miles distant.

My first real work on the home range began with the fall round-up in which we also gathered beef. I had more than the usual interest in this round-up, since it was arranged that I should go east with the beef shipment and spend the winter at school. Short-handed as we were, the work of branding calves and gathering beef in one operation was slow and sufficiently laborious, but when the day came on which we were to leave the range and hit the trail for Miles City, we had a great plenty of riders and horses to make up the trail crew, and the two hundred miles we were to drive were justly regarded as a pleasure trip.

While rounding up the easternmost portion of our range, we picked up four Texas steers. These were the first real Longhorns that I had ever seen, beautiful, trim-built specimens of their breed. We threw them in with our beef herd to be shipped and disposed of for account of the owner of the brand. The presence of these waifs in that remote locality was a mystery which, so far as I was concerned, was not solved until forty years later, when I read Andy Adam's "Log of a Cowboy." The herd of Mexican cattle which he trailed from the Rio Grande to the Blackfoot Reservation skirted the eastern limits of our range, and I am convinced that the four Longhorns that we found were strays from his herd. The Texan quartette were valuable members of the herd, alert, active, and enterprising; they led their more sedate brethren every foot of the way. They were the spear-head of our advance.

There was much of routine about our drive. I was usually selected to ride ahead of the herd and scare away straggling bands of buffalo, so that their behavior might not startle our beef cattle. This does not mean that the country was overrun with them, but a small band of stampeded buffalo could disturb the equanimity of fourteen hundred fat beeves, and one little run would run off a dollar's worth of tallow from each animal. We made two or three dry camps before reaching the Yellowstone. The country traversed was naturally arid, and hardly a drop of rain had fallen since the spring deluge. We managed, however, to find water for our cattle every day but one. This day found us on the dry uplands known as Bull Mountains, and we bedded down our tired herd within five miles of the Yellowstone, after driving from daylight to dark. The cattle were unquiet, as was natural, and extra men were on herd. It was a bright, cold, starlit night, and until one o'clock everything was reasonably quiet and we were congratulating ourselves that we would get through the night without any trouble, when a slight draft of air from the south brought the scent of open water to our thirsty herd. It seemed that every animal was on foot in an instant! There was a low chorus of that kind of bovine talk which cannot be described to anyone who has not heard it, and to him who has, it needs no description. We managed to keep our herd under some kind of restraint for about three hours, when, with the first streak of dawn, they went beyond control, heading in the direction of the desired water. The leaders were belly-deep in the Yellowstone when the drag was still two miles away.

It took a long time for every animal to satisfy his thirst, and this operation was about concluded when from the cliffs on the opposite side of the river came the reverberating reports of a dozen blasts of dynamite where the Northern Pacific construction crews were making ready for their day's work. Our herd left the immediate vicinity in such haste that we lost two miles before they could be stopped. From this point we drove one hundred miles down the river, but every day when we put the cattle into the water we were compelled to handle the inevitable stampede as soon as their thirst was satisfied and association of ideas had time to operate.

One day while I was waiting for the recurrence of this phenomenon I noticed a prostrate cottonwood log from which the bark had fallen. On its smooth bleached surface were carved the names of two members of Custer's Seventh Cavalry, and the date, 1876.

One day the progress of our drive was interrupted while we paused to examine a curious evidence of the precarious character of life on the Yellowstone in bygone days. A natural conical mound dominated an area of grassy bottom land and the mound was surmounted by a squat log structure with a heavy dirt roof. This puzzling erection was about eight feet square and its walls stood no more than two feet above ground. The heavy logs of which it was built were pierced with loop holes, but there was neither door nor window. Fifty yards away on the valley floor was a ruinous log cabin. The little citadel on the hilltop was accessible only through a tunnel from the old cabin and was a stronghold to which the occupants of the cabin might retreat when hard pressed.

After drifting our cattle down the Yellowstone for nine or ten days we reached the crossing place selected, about five miles above Miles City. We had been favored with pleasant weather from the time of leaving the home range, but now the air turned cold and we endured one of those indeterminate fall storms, neither snow nor rain. Early, very early in the morning, we brought our herd to the river bank and began the rather perilous task of crossing the icy Yellowstone. Our cattle had roamed over a range where only small brooks were to be found and they now had to cross a broad, rapid river, clear and cold, a stream that had carried its fleet of steamboats. In preparation for this event each man had selected the horse he thought best suited to the work, but the best judgment was not always displayed. Some of the boys picked their fleetest and most spirited mounts and these were invariably poor performers in the water. I prevailed upon "Tex," the only member of our party who could not swim a stroke, to ride one of my horses whose capacity I had tested upon occasion during the summer, while I rode another animal, worthless for most purposes, but as steady in the water as a ferry boat. Most of us had shed all unnecessary gear, such as six-shooters and belts, *chaparejos*, boots and spurs, but Tex wore his entire regalia, remarking philosophically that he could swim just as well with his six-shooter on as off. Our discarded apparel was loaded into the mess wagon which was to cross the river on the Fort Keogh ferry a few miles below.

The cattle went into the water with considerable reluctance, but the crossing was well chosen and we kept crowding them until the leaders were carried off their feet by the current and the depth of the water. Instead of striking out boldly for the opposite shore, these swimmers would return to our bank of the river, and we were getting nowhere quite rapidly. At this tide of our affairs "Perk" Burnett undertook to set a good example by swimming his horse across in the hope that the cattle would follow. We watched his progress with considerable interest. There was swift current and swimming water for about one hundred yards, and all went well with him until he was nearing the opposite shore, when his horse began to flounder and Perk left the saddle, or rather he attempted to leave it, for his stirrup leathers and tapaderos held his foot imprisoned. For a few minutes it seemed as though the treacherous Yellowstone was about to claim another victim, but man and horse eventually reached the shore some distance below.

Whether the cattle were encouraged by this leadership or not, we soon had them strung out, and a very interesting spectacle it was—fourteen hundred head of beef cattle, unaccustomed to broad water, yet swimming with unerring instinct, their bodies entirely submerged, only heads, horns, and tails visible, clogging the river in a long diagonal toward the opposite bank. The last steer across, we urged our mounts, willing or otherwise, into the chilly water. Being a good swimmer and having recommended my horse, Baldy, to Tex, I kept in position during the swim just below him, and with unfeigned admiration perceived that his cigarette never went out of action.

When we emerged upon firm ground, we were hardly picturesque. Most of us had carried all superfluous clothing turbanwise on our heads. We were all drenched to the armpits, and our wet underclothing was a long time in warming and utterly failed to dry, for a drizzling rain kept us in an uncomfortable state of sogginess. We had considerable difficulty in getting our cattle across the railroad track, one big steer, in fact, going into open revolt. There was only one lasso in the party and only one man with boots and spurs, but despite adverse conditions, the recalcitrant was finally roped and dragged under a trestle and we moved our herd on slowly to the west bank of the Tongue

River, where we expected to meet the wagon with all the comforts of home. The mess wagon, however, was in difficulty. At the ferry landing the four horses had escaped from the nerveless grasp of the cook, and a rider sent out in search of our ambulatory home returned at dark with an ill-assorted lot of provisions carried behind his saddle, and the news that the horses had not been caught. We had built a rousing fire, around which we stood and steamed in the cold drizzle, relieving at intervals the miserable pair who were holding the herd. This performance continued throughout the entire night.

The picture of the myriad sparks hurrying to join their austere sisters, the stars, has been so often pictured that it seems sacrilege to tear away the last shred of romance and declare the fact that the cowboy's fire was ordinarily a small affair of sagebrush, willow twigs, and pungent *bois de vache*. The cowboy's work was done during the long days of summer, commencing before sunrise and ending before sunset, when the feeble flame was carefully extinguished to avoid the danger of prairie fire. On rare occasions when the round-up was weatherbound and there was necessity for drying heat, the campfire of story might be found.

The storm abated towards morning, and the air, keen and crisp, warmed slowly under the autumn sun. By nine o'clock our mess wagon reached us and we soon forgot, or tried to forget, the hardships of the night.

In due course, our cattle were loaded into cars and I accompanied the shipment to Chicago, afterwards returning to my old home in Wisconsin to attend school for the winter.

CHAPTER XXI

I DO CHICAGO

THREE years in Montana had made me aware that the cowboy, with his peculiarly characteristic garb, his hazardous employment, and the setting in which he was so actively engaged, held many picturesque possibilities. I wondered why no artist had portrayed him in camp, at work, or at play. This was long before the days of Remington, while Charley Russell was still drawing grotesque figures for the amusement of his campmates. The success of later artists and the vogue of the cowboy in the moving pictures are proof that my ideas were not far wrong. The picturesque features of our life have been stressed to a point approaching burlesque, not much resembling the cowboy as I knew him at work.

First of all, he was a young man with work to perform. This work was exacting, mixed with considerable danger, with irregular hours and possibilities of great discomfort and fatigue. He received fair compensation for those days, that is to say, forty dollars per month and his board. Punching cows was work, and did not consist solely in justifiable homicide and rescuing distressed maidens. The peculiarities of the cowboy's dress were based upon practical considerations. Beginning with his high-heeled boots. The high heel held his foot from being thrust through the stirrup in the mêlée of a bucking contest. It was also serviceable in "wrestling" calves, the hind leg of the prostrate animal being held forward in the hollow of the boot. The heavy hand-wrought spurs were serviceable as accelerators and were also useful when hooked into the handmade goat-hair cinch, a sort of sheet anchor which has kept more than one man in the saddle when he otherwise would have been thrown. These spurs with their silver inlay and large silver conchas represented twenty-five hard-earned dollars. Assuming a pair of trousers, the cowboy's legs were covered with heavy leather *chaparejos*, plain, serviceable, waterproof, a protection against wind and cold as well as against brush and thorns. He wore a comfortable woolen shirt, sometimes supplemented by a vest, a gaudy silk handkerchief knotted about his neck, not for decoration but to protect a sensitive part of his body from flying ants and other stinging insects and irritating alkali dust of the arid plains. A broadbrimmed, serviceable sombrero protected his head from sun and rain and was commonly anchored in place by two buckskin strings, very useful in our high gales. The heavy weight of a cartridge belt hung easily from his hips when he was mounted, but was quite an encumbrance afoot. He was an unhappy creature, out of his element on foot. Mounted on a good horse, deep seated in a Spanish style stock saddle, anticipating and responding to every motion of his active horse, capable, clear-eyed, and self-reliant, the cowboy of my memory was truly something to be admired.

With all the enthusiasm of my eighteen years, I determined to carry the glad tidings to the art centers of the east and expound the picturesque possibilities to the first painter I should meet, not doubting that he would pack up and follow me west. I carried my outfit as the drummer carries his samples.

When we arrived at the stockyards with our train load of cattle, our work was finished. With my two companions I drifted across South Halsted Street and took lodgings at one of the numerous cheap hotels. This hostelry may be described as a type. It was a two-story frame affair, the lower front a saloon, the floor plentifully sprinkled with sawdust. Behind this was a dark, dirty dining room, supported, buttressed, and perfumed by a kitchen in the rear. Upstairs were five or six ill-kept bedrooms. These tawdry inns rejoiced in such

From this temporary abode I set forth with two purposes in mind.

names as, "Colorado Hotel," "El Paso House," "The Yellowstone," and "Cowboy's Resort."

From this temporary abode, I set forth with two purposes in mind: I wanted a holster for my pistol, and more important, I was in search of an artist who would portray and interpret for the effete East the story of the West. Never was mission more fatuous! Picture South Halsted Street in the fall of 1882: an overcast autumnal sky, an atmosphere heavy with the stench of stockyards not ameliorated by the odors from the filthy street, and, wending his hesitating way up this thoroughfare, the serio-comic figure of an eighteen-year-old cowboy with high-heeled boots and a sombrero, scanning the signs on the cheap buildings, carrying in his hand, carefully wrapped in newspaper, his faithful and formidable Colts peacemaker, to be fitted, if you please.

I invaded, one after another, the top floor "studios," to find the "artist" a flagrant faker in the tin-type trade. Before noon it was evident to me that my message was destined not to be delivered, or at least it would die "a-borning." I could not believe that my other errand would be equally ill-fated and I climbed the rickety stairs to the "Great Western Leather Works," weary, but hopeful. I found myself outside a broad-topped railing in a large room filled with industrious, pallid workers of both sexes. To the manager I explained my requirements, showing him the weapon and its worn holster. He seemed very much interested, as did his foreman, two or three callers, and as many operatives as could find excuse for leaving their work and coming to the front. But I noted the interest seemed centered in my pearl-handled pistol, and when I left the place, defeated and discouraged, it was after the discovery that the "Great Western Leather Works" confined its activities to the manufacture of ladies' purses and other hen-skin products.

I was now reduced to the condition of an empty cartridge. I had no mission in life. I wandered about the streets, my farthest north being somewhere near the river. I drifted eastward to the Lake Front and sat down for a time to relieve my tired feet. I grew weary of shop windows and made various attempts to find my way homeward, feeling badly confused as to direction. There was no sun to guide me and I was reluctant to ask my way. At length I saw a street car, a horse-drawn contrivance bearing the legend "South Halsted Street," but hopelessly crowded. It served merely as a guide to my direction and I struggled through the crowded sidewalks southward. Each car going my way was more crowded than the last. If there seemed to be a chance for me to get on, the car was sighted in the middle of the block and escaped from me. The way seemed interminable and I was ready to drop with fatigue when I managed to board a car which was fairly empty. I had no more than surrendered my nickel than the car stopped, and I discovered that I had been landed at the end of the line—the stockyards at my right, the desired "hotel" at my left.

I arrived at the old home on a Sunday morning. I had brought with me as baggage, my cowboy outfit, but my hand baggage was enclosed in a blanket-covered roll gripped in a shawl strap. I wore my cowboy hat and high-heeled boots and an ill-fitting hand-me-down suit. I was much changed by thirty months' absence, but the old town was the same. I exulted in my incognito, while I sentimentalized over familiar faces and places. Boyish fancies of invisibility were being, in a measure, realized. I passed the fire engine house. Johnson, promoted to engineer in the department, knew me not. Other acquaintances scrutinized my strange figure with a greater or less affectation of good breeding, but with no recognition. I neared the little church at which I had been such a faithful attendant, and only one touch was necessary to make me feel that I was really at home. This was not wanting, for Dr. Chase's dog ran to the fence and barked savagely. This was his custom, but not content with keeping within bounds, he crossed the property line and threatened something more serious than noise. In self-defense I swung my bundled luggage at his head and he withdrew in ignominious defeat, for out of the bundle he had been showered, as if by shrapnel, with a navy revolver, a pair of spurs, a cartridge belt, and the scattered contents of a box of .45 cartridges. While I was engaged in "mopping up" the sidewalk, the church doors opened, and my old playmates and associates with their staid elders were upon me. I will confess to considerable embarrassment, but I was not recognized. It was no wonder, I had left the congregation less than three years before a well-mannered, well-dressed, pale and thoughtful boy, and I had come back as brown as an Indian, three inches taller, and clad in outlandish garb, from my high-heeled boots to my exotic sombrero. Who could imagine Johnny Barrows on his hands and knees gathering up implements of death from the sidewalk, almost at the door of Zion Church on a Sunday morning? Another block brought me to the welcome shelter of the home of my uncle, John Rumsey.

For a short time after my arrival I was the center of considerable interest. I brought direct news from many who had left the old town to court fortune in the remote West, and the curiosity of the stay-at-homes had to be satisfied. With companions of my own age I was quite at ease, and had much to relate. In explanation of some of my stories it was necessary that I should demonstrate my skill with the lasso. I roped a dog in front of the post office and got my name in the newspaper. The young fry robbed their mother's clotheslines and with their makeshift lassos every bossy-cow in town was fringed. Such fame, however, is ephemeral. After being the talk of the town for about a week, I soon settled down to the serious business of the winter—attending school.

CHAPTER XXII

LIFE ON THE DHS

HE spring of '83 found me again employed on the DHS ranch, where I was beginning to feel much at home. In Granville Stuart, part owner and manager of this outfit, I had found a man who so commanded my respect and admiration that his influence upon my character and conduct was profound. A Virginian by descent, one of the earliest of Montana's pioneers, an instinctive gentleman, self-educated, well-read, fearless; a man who had married a Shoshone squaw who held her place in his household as a loved and respected wife and mother—he needed no other qualities to make him my ideal. Under the mud roof of his log cabin library there were housed several thousand volumes of good books, and in this library, whenever opportunity offered, I obtained my substitute for an education. Such friendship as is sometimes shown between a veteran and a youngster existed between us, never broken to the day of his death. My hours in the library were not always devoted to reading. A rack of firearms, obsolete and modern, was the starting point of many vivid accounts of pioneer experiences dating back to 1857 when the flintlock was the common arm of the Indian, and Colt's muzzle-loading revolver the latest thing in fire-arms. In explaining the mutilation of a Hudson's Bay "fuke," he gave a dramatic account of the first buffalo chase he had witnessed on an early visit from western Montana to the plains country. A small hunting party of Blackfeet was running a herd of buffalo and shooting with such rapidity that Stuart was sure they were armed with some kind of repeating or breech-loading rifles, but he found that the untutored savage had devised a method for converting his crude flintlock trade gun into a rapid fire weapon by an ingenious but simple process. In order that the long clumsy musket might be used in one hand, the barrel was filed off, reducing its length nearly one-half. The stock was similarly amputated and the result might be called an immense, clumsy horse pistol. To avoid the necessity of opening the pan and priming it at every shot the touch hole was reamed out to a generous size. With horse at full gallop, the possessor of this remarkable weapon poured into the muzzle an unmeasured charge of powder, and upon this haphazard explosive spat, from a supply carried in his mouth, one large, round, leaden ball which fitted so loosely in the generous bore of the musket that it settled into place without the aid of a ramrod. The gun was carried muzzle up during all this performance and until the moment of discharge, priming itself through the enlarged touch hole. Thus prepared, the Indian hunter had only to urge his horse to the approved position alongside the running buffalo, when the weapon was pointed and discharged in one motion. There could be no possibility of missing, but there was the everpresent chance that the gun might burst.

In the early years of my Montana experience nearly every man and boy was armed for protection against the Indians. Compared with other sections of the West, there was little outlawry in the eastern foothills of Montana. Cowboys and men who were much in the saddle usually contented themselves with the favorite navy revolver, Colt's .45, the "peacemaker," serviceable, accurate, and powerful. This was loosely housed in a heavy, open-top leather scabbard, looped upon a cartridge belt. This was often supplemented by a Winchester model '73 carbine, slung in its leather holster under the right knee.

The hunter was variously armed according to special preference or the character of his game. The muzzle-loading rifle had been retired and in its place could be found the Winchester rifles '73 and '76 as well as their prototype, the Henry. The single-shot rifles, commonly favored for heavy game were Sharp's "Old Reliable," the "Ballard," and the Springfield "needle gun." The weapon with which I became most familiar was Colt's navy revolver. With it, as the result of assiduous practice, I became more than reasonably expert. Its length from firing pin to muzzle end was about nine inches. It carried a heavy bullet and as much powder as could be burned in its length of barrel. This was usually carried with only five chambers loaded, the hammer resting upon the empty chamber to avoid accidents so common in roping, when the hammer might be lifted by a tightening rope across the hip. Speaking broadly, the cowboys were expert with their revolvers. The open-top holster facilitated quick action in drawing, the gun was promptly elevated, and, as it was dropped to aim, the hammer was brought to full cock, smoothly and almost automatically, by the well-trained thumb. The trigger mechanism was commonly *doctored* until the slightest touch would release the hammer. The revolver was held loosely, and its unchecked recoil raised it and the hand into position for the next shot. Where the accuracy of the rifle was needed for a distant target, the revolver marksman would commonly seat himself upon the ground and hold the revolver with both hands, resting his elbows upon his flexed knees.

CHAPTER XXIII

I ACQUIRE A CAYUSE

T THIS time I traded the first horse I could really call my own for Kid, the saddle horse of my fond memories, whom I would gladly meet in the happy hunting grounds. Billy, whom I traded, was a dour morose cayuse of doubtful paternity. I acquired him as a suckling in exchange for some services in Gaugler's trading post. Upon my return from Wisconsin, Billy was three years old, wild and insubordinate. The contest between us was Homeric. In his bucking, whatever he lacked in technical ability was fully compensated by his energy and stubbornness. For nearly half an hour the contest raged between us in a very restricted area. He would not run, reserving all his powers for pitching. He bucked until he was tired and then stood, sullen and laboring for breath, until he regained his strength for another attempt. It detracted a little from my glory that I strained my right arm in clutching the saddle horn, but the soreness was gone in a matter of two weeks, while I never lost the confidence engendered by this, my first successful attempt at broncho busting. But Billy, subdued and shaped into a serviceable saddle horse, was not to my liking, and my trade for Kid gave me immense satisfaction. Kid was small, compact, short-backed, with high withers and long hips. He was distinctly a short distance horse. From a standing start, for two hundred yards or so, he could beat almost anything I ever rode, but that was sufficient in his opinion to give me my chance with the lasso. In color he was dapple gray, very uncommon in those days among saddle horses, and he was as intelligent and affectionate as horses of that color were reputed to be. Perfection is not of this world, and Kid's fault was that he was gun-shy. Only once did this fault make me think regretfully of Billy, and that was one day when we were plodding through deep snow, five miles from home. With the reins on his neck, I pulled a bandana from my hip pocket and instantly measured my length on the snow, still holding the handkerchief between my thumb and forefinger, whereupon I *walked* the five miles home.

Our horses were commonly called "cayuses," which need not imply that they were brought from the Pacific slope, the home of the Cayuse Indians. Of Spanish origin, hardiness had been developed by Nature's inexorable law, under severe range conditions and the mismanagement of Indians.

Except for the effect of the law of survival, little had been done to change or improve the breed. In comparison with the "American" horse he was small, compact, hardy, and wild, with sound lungs and good feet, very satisfactory for our work, where nimbleness and toughness were required, but he was almost worthless as a draft animal. Beyond the necessary attention in the corral at branding time he knew no allegiance nor control until he was three years old, when the horse band, headed by the imperious and often dangerous stallion, was driven from the hills, and with the tightening of the lasso, he found his freedom at an end.

His first lessons in the seriousness of life and his duty to man might be received at the hands of a professional *vaquero,* or a broncho buster, for many well-qualified riders devoted themselves to horse breaking. Or he might be turned over to the cowboy who was to ride him for the season, or for years. At all events, half strangled, snorting, trembling and enraged, he was first subjected to the indignity of a *jaquima,* or "hackamore." This was a very effective braided rawhide halter, with a hard rounded noseband placed low enough so that a severe pull would close the cayuse's nostrils. Next a blind, made from the leather of an old boot leg, or improvised from a handkerchief, was placed over his eyes and completed the impotency of the unhappy colt, left him standing with braced legs, sweating with excitement, powerless to resent the crowning insult of the saddle. This was the time to leave him to his melancholy thoughts, and smoke a cigarette. The blind was usually lifted in the corral and resulted in an outburst of futile but enthusiastic bucking, varied with energetic kicks at the dangling stirrups. This first outbreak concluded, the victim led or herded out of the corral was again blinded and with due caution, mounted. It was customary to employ a herder in the first riding, a mounted companion, who in various skillful ways encouraged the colt to run, or upon occasion fairly crowded the terrified beast out of dangerous corners. The colt's ineffectual attempts to rid himself of the saddle were seldom sufficient to discourage a very thorough effort to unseat the rider, but sooner or later he would give up pitching and attempt to run away from his trouble. If he headed east, he might run for five hundred miles without striking a fence or a human habitation, but in any direction there was room enough for him to exhaust his energies, and in two hours he might be looked for, returning with lowered head and uncertain gait to the corral, a "broke horse." So far as the rider was concerned, and depending upon his skill and strength, he might be weary or ready for another broncho. The professionals would call this session one-fifth of a day's work, but the ordinary cow hand, with only one or two colts to break, would call this a day and be ready to ride the half-subdued animal on the morrow, when he would be considered broken for the work of riding the circle.

CHAPTER XXIV

BRONCHO BUSTING

RONCHO busting from another angle leads to consideration o f t h e rider's point of view, which would naturally vary with the individual, according to his experience and skill, or lack of these qualities. I mounted my first broncho, debonair and complacent. My second attempt, after a year and a half of preparation, found me faltering and filled with doubts. It was only my determination to master that feature of the cowboy's work that enabled me to subdue my real physical fears and undertake the contest. After four or five years in the saddle and a fair amount of experience with bronchos and spoiled horses, I had attained a proficiency in riding which made the breaking of a colt almost a matter of routine. Riding a broncho was the diversion of a Sunday afternoon.

If broncho busting could be called a sport it must necessarily be qualified by the adjective "strenuous," as it was undoubtedly both dangerous and exciting. The horses were almost as wild as the deer and the antelope with which they grazed. They were muscular and agile, they were likely to bite, strike, kick, or throw themselves backward. They were certain to buck and they testified to their rage and terror by a most infernal bawling and squealing. The run, after the first pitching, was anything but monotonous, for at any moment the extended leap of the running horse might change into an energetic frenzy of bucking. If the rider let the colt have his head he bucked harder. If by any means his head was held up he was the more likely to fall or throw himself backwards. Riding wild horses may safely be called an occupation for young men who wish to enliven a monotonous life and are not especially anxious to lengthen it.

One hot summer day our round-up was in camp on Blood Creek, near the eastern limit of our range. If my memory serves me, a half dozen men had gone with two wagons to the mountains for corral poles. Those of us who remained in camp were enjoying a holiday after our job of digging post-holes had been completed. There was one member of our group who was a misfit as a cowboy, but was one of us by virtue of his kinship with one of the owners. He was a fair rider and conceited enough to think that he was worthy of a higher classification. After considerable banter, he was challenged to demonstrate his skill by riding our one-eyed pack horse, "Good-eye." Good-eye had been mishandled in breaking and had developed into what we called a spoiled horse; he would buck whenever ridden. As the cowboy in those ancient days had work to do and no audience to entertain, a spoiled horse was about as popular as is faulty ignition in these automobile days, so we found another field of usefulness for Good-eye; we converted him into a pack horse, when it was discovered that he did not buck in that service.

The day herder caught the horse and brought him into camp. He was saddled and bridled and the contest was only delayed while a few modest wagers were arranged. We were lounging in the shade of the box elders in the little valley of the Bad Land stream, and there in our very midst the contest was held, for Good-eye was known to be businesslike rather than impetuous and coltish. The rider mounted, seated himself in the saddle, and touched his spurs to Good-eye's ribs. The horse took the hint and gave us a very interesting exhibition of bucking, an exhibition featuring energy, skill, and experience, but quite devoid of passion. He did not cover much ground, he did not change ends, nor sunfish, but he had a remarkable retrograde action. The rider was loosened with the first jump, he lost his stirrups at the second, at the third he got an ultra-violent raise, and at the fourth he landed astride Good-eye's withers, ahead of the saddle, just as the horse stopped bucking and raised his head.

All was quiet, the storm was over; the horse turned his good eye toward us with a glance that was puzzled and benign. *Our* interest was centered in the predicament of the rider. It is difficult to imagine a situation more embarrassing. He could not get back into the saddle, there was no relief in front, but the feature which contributed most to the comedy of the situation was the behavior of Good-eye, who stood perfectly still, imperturable and docile, as if the situation contained no novel feature. Our laughter was riotous. I never saw anything so funny in a long experience. We encouraged and advised the rider, we argued the question as to who had won in the contest and in this argument the discomfited rider, from his precarious and uncomfortable position, made special plea and contended that he had not been thrown. Whereupon he was asked to dismount, which was quite impossible. All he could do was to fall off, which he finally did, continuing the argument amidst much laughter, until finally all bets were declared off.

I cannot pass over the season of '83 without some reference to our camp cook, an expatriated Scot named John McKeown. He had reached the advanced age of perhaps forty, and in consequence and in evidence of our affection for him was known as "Old Johnny." He was a hopeless slave to liquor, and we had to herd him and his mess wagon through every settlement where liquor could be obtained, but he was a good fellow and a good cook. He drove a fiery team of four outlaw horses, spoiled in the breaking, but willing to perform in harness. His mess wagon was a three-inch Schuttler, with a double box and excellent canvas cover well stretched over the bows. The rear end of this wagon was replaced by a well-built cupboard the exact width of the wagon box and about four feet high. The broad door to this cupboard, hinged at the bottom, could be lowered, discovering the cupboard contents stowed on their shelves, and it served as the cook's table. The forward part of the wagon carried the bulk of our provisions, sacks of flour, sides of bacon, sugar, hominy, rice, and beans, dried apples and peaches in boxes, canned tomatoes in cases (the only canned goods furnished), and perhaps a small supply of potatoes. In order that our commissary department might be self-contained, this wagon carried also the cook tent with its poles and gear.

In moving from corral to corral, or from camp to camp on the trail, Johnny with his outfit and the driver of the bed wagon who hauled with almost similar equipment the bedding, tents, branding irons, and so forth, piloted their caravan over untracked prairie, through unbridged streams, down and up ungraded hills, to destinations sometimes unknown, or indicated in the morning by a pointed finger and two or three words descriptive. At noon we would find Old Johnny fully established and at home, with a satisfying hot meal ready for our unqualified appetites. The well-known trials and tribulations of a camp cook were his, but he had the knack of surmounting and minimizing them.

Once I saw him thoroughly whipped. It was between round-ups, about eleven o'clock on a hot July day, when news was brought to the ranch that the Indians had killed a number of cattle on lower Ford Creek, something more than thirty miles distant. The horse herd was brought in with a rush resembling a stampede. The company carbines with their scabbards and ammunition were distributed, saddles were thrown upon our long distance horses and while Johnny threw a small supply of provisions into his yawning cupboard, his horses were hooked up and we galloped down the valley in a cloud of dust. Whenever we glanced back we could see the galloping cayuses and the reeling lumber wagon close behind. We had about

Whenever we glanced back we could see the galloping cayuses and the reeling chuck wagon close behind.

two hours of this before we came upon the dead cattle and saw in one glance that they had been killed by lightning. At this juncture Johnny drove up and stopped his lathered horses on a perfect camp site under the cottonwoods, a picture of triumph. But his exultation fell from him like a mantle, when he discovered that his cupboard door had jogged open during the wild ride and his shelves were as bare as Old Mother Hubbard's. Here indeed was calamity! We had our bedding and a fifty-pound sack of flour, an axe, and a shovel. There was some debate about returning, but we had run the tails off our horses already, and thirty-five miles up hill did not appeal to us. We compromised by killing a calf, baking unleavened bread upon the shovel, and drinking alkali water. The roasted meat was delicious, though lacking salt.

CHAPTER XXV

YARNS

FORT MAGINNIS, less than three miles from the DHS ranch was the local metropolis, and the post-trader's store was our base of supplies. But the thriving mining camp of Maiden, seven miles away over the crest of the Judith Mountains was more popular. There was less restraint, a freedom from military red tape, and always a possibility that something might happen. Thither we trooped in the lazy weeks between round-ups, thence we returned and it often happened upon our return that I, being sober and the others not so much so, carried the artillery equipment of the entire detachment hung over my saddle horn. I had no desire to be eccentric and I had read no tract about the "demon rum," but I had seen his work, and my experiences in the "deadfall" at the forks of the Musselshell had convinced me that whiskey was good stuff to leave alone.

The fall and beef round-ups were devoid of special interest although such work can hardly be described as humdrum. I did not accompany the outfit on the beef drive as it was no part of my plan to make another trip east. Upon my return to Ubet I took up the duties of the winter, multifarious, but not exacting. I had a few colts to break, I performed most of the duties of the postmaster, and our post office was rather important, being at the junction of the lines from White Sulphur Springs to Fort Maginnis and from Billings to Fort Benton. The Billings-Benton line handled considerable traffic and was equipped with four-horse Concord coaches and very decent stock. Many of the drivers were old timers who had seen better days before the railroad era and voiced their humiliation at driving four horses instead of six, unaware that in a few years some of them would be driving a team to a spring wagon, for the stagecoach days were passing.

At this time I had a local reputation as an idler, due to the fact that I spent much time in reading, but I had the general management of our little herd of cattle, forty or fifty head, and upon occasions had to look after our small band of horses. In addition I was the handy man of the local blacksmith, and did my share of extra work in the store and saloon.

Ubet is situated in a stormy section. The Judith Gap is a draughty place, and quite often after a blizzard coming in from the north had blown itself out, we would experience what was known locally as a Gap wind blowing back from the south, and quite as disagreeable as the blizzard. But Montana winter is made tolerable by periods of calm weather with moderate or warm temperatures and bright skies. At such times we saw to it that everything was prepared for the coming of the next storm. In the coldest weather our outside activities were reduced to a minimum, and we limited our operations to the necessary chores. At such times we had long hours around a glowing stove and told and retold our adventures and misadventures.

One evening our chatter seemed to run to humiliations, and almost every member of our group had some incident to relate in which he had played an inglorious part. It was a time for confessions. Bill Newton, who happened to be stormbound with us, told a story which I believe he had never told before.

"While we are exchanging confessions," he began, "I'll tell you about the hardest fall I ever got. Three years ago I was coming down from Fort Benton and I stayed over night at old Colonel Viall's place on Wolf Creek. Next morning I saddled up and started out for Ubet.

"The weather was just what the doctor ordered, the sun was just warm enough, the old grass had been burnt off the year before and the new growth made the country so green that Ireland would look plumb yellow beside it. Everything was just exactly right. I had a good breakfast inside of me, I had a good horse, and I couldn't find fault with my outfit. There was no wind, just a little breeze, not a cloud in the sky and the mountains all around were perfectly satisfactory; the Snowies, the Judiths, and the Moccasins looked like scenery that had been painted to order. Actually I began to feel silly, like those fellows who write poetry.

"When I rode out of the Sage Creek valley onto the bench, I saw that there was something ahead of me and I let my horse have his head to catch up. Pretty soon I was alongside of the darndest looking outfit that I ever saw. It was a sheep herder on a little whittle-dy-dig of a long-tail pony. Now you know my opinion of sheep herders. When a man gets so worthless that he can't fish floaters out of a swill barrel, he goes to herding sheep. Well, this fellow was a sheep herder, I could tell by the smell. The whole outfit was like a bad dream. He was kind of undersized, with a harmless face; his hair was long, and he wore a Buffalo Bill mustache and goatee. He had on one of those English hunting caps with a peak in front and behind (they are all right if a man doesn't know whether he is coming or going), and it had kind of gores in the sides, so that it could be laced up or let out, so that it would fit your head next morning.

"He had a decent old saddle, but his stirrups weren't mates and he wore shoes, the kind that have elastic on the sides, and his pants had worked up and his socks down. The whole outfit was a crime, but the queerest thing, according to my notion, was the way the man was built. He was kind of spindling, but he had a bay window that filled the saddle from cantle to horn. Do you know, I kind of enjoyed riding alongside of this freak? I would take one look at him and then I would kind of stand off at one side and look at myself.

"Of course we were talking as we rode along together, and my curiosity kept growing; no matter what I was talking about, I kept thinking of his circumference and trying to calculate his diameter at the equator. Now I despise sheep herders, but I didn't want to be too rough with this fellow, so I said, 'What tree is that saddle you're riding?' He said, 'It's a long Frieseke.' I knew that but I asked him how long it was. He says, 'It's an eighteen-inch seat.' 'You fill it pretty well,' says I. He agreed with me and I went on, 'You must have punished lots of good grub in your time.' He put one hand on his Tropic of Capricorn and looked at me kind of sad and said, 'This is the result of accident.' 'Accident?' said I, 'blowed up, maybe?' This seemed so darned good to me that I said it again, 'I guess you was blowed up?' 'No,' said he, 'it wasn't an explosion; it was accidental substitution.' Well, of course I kept on worming around until he told me about it.

"He said that when he was a kid he had taken a job in a sawmill where they worked him almost to death and he didn't get any decent grub. Finally he quit and went home to his folks, and the first meal he ate there tasted so good and he was so hungry that he stuffed himself with good things and then went to bed. After a while he waked up with a horrible bellyache; and while he was telling me how he suffered, the old reprobate took out a red cotton handkerchief and wiped his eyes and went on. 'The pain was perfectly intolerable, and finally I got up and went to the medicine closet. I knew just exactly where we kept that bottle of "Perry Davis's Pain Killer," and I found it in the dark and I rubbed myself for about an hour.' 'Didn't it blister you?' said I. 'No,' he said, 'I wish it had. It wasn't "Pain Killer" at all. We had a skinny hired girl working for us that summer and I had got hold of her bottle of "Bustine Guaranteed Permanent." '

"I just took one look at him and then I touched my old horse with the spur, just ahead of the cinch, and said, 'Well, I guess I must be going,' and I rode through to the Gap without stopping."

CHAPTER XXVI

NIGHT HERDING

THE coming of the spring of 1884 did not seem to me like the termination of a long vacation, as I shipped my bedding and saddled Kid to resume my work on the DHS ranch. After considerable debate with myself, I undertook the work of night herding the horses for the summer. Our round-up had "by little and little" grown to respectable size. New outfits had driven to the range; the territory covered was much larger than in the days when the DHS was the only brand, and it was proposed to have the round-up horses, about two hundred in number, night herded by two men. At this work I had had considerable experience and rather preferred it to any other feature of the business. It had the advantage of short hours, also the night hawk escaped the heat and dust of the corral and the annoyance of insect pests, at least during his eight hours on duty. Nights were short in our northern latitude and the pay was higher. The individual selected for my side partner in this work was a discharged infantryman from Fort Maginnis, city bred, with no horse experience. We were somewhat appalled the first evening of the round-up to observe that he attempted to put his horse's bridle on hind side before, and that, preparatory to mounting, he inserted his foot in the front of the stirrup. The first night's herding with a fresh aggregation of horses was rather hard work, in which I received little help. Our second night was dark and cloudy and my assistant was dreadfully seasick during most of the time, complaining that his horse bobbing up and down in the dark affected him. If he was filled with nausea, I was filled with disgust, and on the following day I undertook to herd the horses alone in consideration of a substantial increase in my pay. That summer I was undoubtedly the highest paid night herder in Montana.

The occasional discomforts of our life could be borne only by youngsters who fancied they were a necessary part of a glorious career, or by hardened veterans who knew no other way of life. As I can speak feelingly for the night herder, let me give you what the anatomist calls a "frozen section" of a rainy day on a round-up. In his damp bed at the rear of the tent the night herder tries to get the few hours sleep which are absolutely necessary. So far as sleep is concerned the night hawk has no reserve, he is always "busted." The tent is slatting in the wind; an occasional drop falls upon his face; his companions, a dozen or more, are with him in the tent, killing time to their individual tastes. There is occasional target practice with the big .45's from the tent door, and altogether the long day may bring him very little sleep. Promptly, you may be sure, the day herder will bring in the dripping herd of horses and the night herder catches his horse for the long vigil. Almost invariably the horse has recently rolled to quiet the intolerable itching of his back, and the first step is to scrape his back carefully with a mop of sagebrush. The sulky and unhappy brute is now comforted with a damp saddle blanket and the unwelcome saddle. The night hawk's attention is now turned to the condition of his boots, which are daubed and plastered with gumbo and dead grass till they are larger and heavier than any wooden shoe. At last, in some fashion, he is mounted and goes out into the gloom for the eight long hours of solitary blackness, pelted by the cold rain, riding perhaps on the flank of a wild stampede at a thundering gallop over country absolutely unseen, or perhaps subject only to the steady unhappiness of a wet saddle seat and quite unable to make a smoke. Repeat this for three or four nights and you will convince most individuals that there is no place like home.

UBET

After making a brief dash to work the debatable ground to our north with the Moccasin round-up we hurried seventy miles south to work the borderland east of the Snowies with the Musselshell round-up. Here we gathered together one hundred and twenty-five riders and their mounts, probably eight or nine hundred head of horses, a combining of the upper Musselshell, lower Musselshell and DHS round-ups, as well as representatives from the Yellowstone and other ranges. It was indeed a "whale of a round-up." We branded in corrals and we branded casually on the prairie in living corrals formed by twenty or thirty riders. The morning circle enclosed an empire of territory.

Our work upon adjoining ranges finished, we returned to the initial corral near the DHS ranch and began to work on familiar ground. We were a well-organized, homogeneous party, a small but effective round-up unit, dominated of course by the DHS brand which covered more than three-fourths of the cattle on the range, but moving in efficient fashion under this leadership. There were twenty-five or thirty riders, three outfits with their cooks, and one man who drove the tent wagon for this outfit and made himself generally useful as a satellite of Johnny McKeown, while I had the proud distinction of being the only night hawk.

At about eight o'clock, long before dark, I would

take over the herd of horses from the day herder
and allow my charges to select their own grazing
ground, if their choice was not too far from camp.
For a couple of hours, or until daylight had almost
entirely vanished from the northwest, there was
very industrious nibbling with the indescribable
equine sounds of satisfaction and good feeling. I
assume the night to be clear, calm, and crisp, the
sky luminous with the nearby stars of high alti-
tudes. Except for the pleasant sounds from the
grazing herd, nothing disturbs the stillness but
the occasional song of the coyote or the plaint of
some disturbed meadowlark. About ten o'clock it
is time to put on an overcoat and see that the herd
is kept slowly moving to embarrass those irregular
individuals who would like to snore in the early
part of the night and graze later, to the detriment
of herd discipline. By half past twelve the entire
herd is full, contented, and ready for sleep. Perhaps half of the band will lie down, while others
cat nap on foot in lounging attitudes with an occasional comic snore.

For nearly two hours, I may lounge at ease in
the saddle and devote my intellect to the settling of
all vexed questions in philosophy, religion, or
science, but with the coming of an ivory tint on the
eastern clouds, the horses renew their interminable
occupation of grazing, and require some herding.

At four o'clock I rout out the cooks; about a quarter of an hour later, allowing something less than ten minutes for a cowboy toilet, I ride through the camp, beating my heavy quirt upon the tightened canvas of the tents to arouse the riders. Our two wagons, end to end, form one side of an improvised corral. From the rear wheel of the rear wagon and the front wheel of the other, long ropes are stretched and held breast high. The ropes are shaken vigorously and thus become about as effective as a ten-pole corral. The riders, with ready lasso, stand along the open side of this make-shift enclosure. Two hundred head of horses, partly broken and broncho, are closely bunched before them. It may be imagined that to identify and lasso a selected individual from this herd is somewhat difficult, but it is speedily accomplished. The horses are so closely crowded together that their heads are held high. The bronchos keep the herd in a state of ebullition and with almost unerring precision the small loops are "pitched" a distance of thirty or forty feet around the neck of the desired animal.

One morning when we were in camp at Button Butte, I drove my horse herd into the open corral and one of the first men to pitch a rope failed to get the horse intended, and caught instead a broncho, by the neck and shoulders. The affrighted beast broke out of the herd and could not be held. I was riding Flapjacks, a little cow pony so called on account of his peculiar build, deep draft, and small beam. He was a veteran, an adept, carrying upon his scarred hide brands reminiscent of experiences ranging from the Panhandle of Texas to Montana. I started in immediate pursuit of the escaping animal, which ran down into a creek valley, a difficult piece of ground with a deep meandering stream five or six feet in width, complicated by a newly dug irrigation ditch. My horse, in hot pursuit, leaped the creek, and simultaneously, the broad brim of my hat (a nerveless thing that I had dubbed a Gainsborough, for it was no sombrero) blew down into my face, effectually blinding me. As I lifted my quirt hand to raise the blind, Flapjacks, in ardent chase, made a quick turn which nearly unseated me and I grabbed the horn of the saddle, or as we used to phrase it, "went for leather." After two or three jumps in a direct line I was sufficiently secure in the saddle to make another attempt to raise my hat brim, but Flapjacks, intent upon his quarry, whirled suddenly and jumped the ditch. This manoeuver caused me to lose both stirrups and when he had again turned, leaping the ditch for the second time, it required all the strength I had in both arms to keep from going overboard. There followed a most bewildering and exciting time, with Flapjacks in sole command. I was a mere passenger. How many times the wise old horse jumped the ditch or creek I do not know. When he finally stopped and I was able to raise the flapping hat brim from my eyes, the broncho was back in the corral, and Flapjacks wore a well-earned air of conscious merit.

CHAPTER XXVII

ROUND-UP

O NE by one the captive mounts for the morning ride are led out, saddled, bridled and tied to wagon wheels. My work is now finished, but the day herder sits down to breakfast with us, with an occasional glance at the loose horses which have trotted out of camp limits and may demand his attention before he reaches the bread and molasses stage.

Breakfast is soon dispatched. Captain Bill Burnett is mounted and lighting his first cigarette. Selecting his leaders by name, he directs one to take two men and drive the country drained by a certain water course; to another he assigns a half dozen riders to cover a different territory, and so on until an area which may cover three hundred square miles has been allotted. These little parties, leaving camp in divergent directions, gallop smartly for distances ranging from five to fifteen miles, until they have reached the periphery of the rude circle. There, separating, as individuals they begin the return journey to the cutting-out ground near the corral.

[191]

UBET

The cattle, almost as wild as their predecessors, the buffalo, when first sighted will run for two or three miles. Small herds of fifteen or twenty come streaming out of the lush pastures of the ravines and join the larger bodies. There is much bellowing, and the shouts of the cowboys, together with an occasional harmless pistol shot, contribute to the idea of motion. When the cattle have moved five miles or so on a hot morning, they will require some urging. There will be distracted mothers looking for the calves they had seen but a moment before; surly, defiant bulls who require attention; but the herd, augmented as it moves, is nearing its destination, and arrived, is usually willing to take a little rest. Two men will be left on herd while the others gallop to camp, release their sweating horses and sit down to dinner. By this time I will have absorbed my six-hour portion of sleep in the willows by the creek and, somewhat drowsy, I take my share of the midday meal. The day herder brings in the horse herd; well-trained horses for cutting out and roping are caught and saddled, and the afternoon work begins.

Two or three skillful riders enter the herd, moving about as quietly as possible, and cut out cows with young unbranded calves. These can be worked to the edge of the herd with little trouble, but are often difficult to drive out. Soon,

Two ropers ride in with the cattle. The bars are closed.

however, a "cut" is formed of cows and calves already driven out, and the selected ones are not at all reluctant to move from one herd to another. When all the mothers of one brand and their unmarked calves have been cut out, they are driven into the corral, a substantial circular pen perhaps sixty feet in diameter. Outside this corral the fire has been blazing merrily, the irons are hot. Two ropers ride in with the cattle, the bars are closed; four calf "wrastlers" tie their horses to the corral, and, working in pairs, throw and hold the bawling, struggling calves as the ropers drag them from the huddle of frightened animals in the enclosure. The brander comes with his hot iron; there is a suffocating smoke from the burning hair; some struggling outcry from the helpless victim, who is quickly ear-marked or otherwise treated by the pseudo-surgeon with a reasonably sharp jackknife, and the elder, perched on the corral top, sings out, "one heifer," or "one steer" and makes an entry in his tally book.

It is impossible to describe the rapidity with which this work is done by a good crew under favorable circumstances. The roper is so certain to catch his calf with the first throw, that a good corral horse, without guidance, will start for the fire as soon as the rope is thrown, and shows unmistakable signs of disgust if he finds that he is not dragging a struggling calf behind him; the "wrastlers," with perfect team work, throw the calf and release the lasso in the twinkling of an eye. With equal celerity the other operations are performed. All calves branded, the corral is ready for the next cut of a different brand, until finally the slick-ears or mavericks (orphans unbranded and of indeterminate ownership) are auctioned and branded under pool arrangement. Meanwhile the herd is uneasy, hungry, and homesick. The bulls, unquestioned lords of their own harems, thus summarily brought together, have fought and decided innumerable questions of precedence. With the last cut, the main herd is released to start in some confusion for their home range. The riders return to camp, the fire is quenched, the irons are cooling. A choice two-year-old is butchered, and his hind quarters apportioned to the different messes. The hide will be left on the ground unless needed for lasso making and the forequarters will be poisoned for the ubiquitous coyote.

In the long days of the spring round-up the sun will still be high at the finish of the evening meal. Sunset will find some of the riders in bed and the day herder anxiously consulting his cheap watch, while I am preparing for my lonely vigil with the horse herd.

UBET

The next day, to come so soon, may be a replica of yesterday, with the difference that the branding will be at another corral, perhaps fifteen miles distant, and the riders who drove from the most distant part of the new circle will have a ride of twenty-five miles before they commence their real work of gathering cattle. Ordinarily we devoted one day to each corral and this involved moving camp each day. The tents were taken down, bedding neatly rolled and tied, and every convenience or necessity of our portable home would be loaded into the wagons for transfer to the new location. Sometimes the wagons followed a well-defined trail from camp to camp; sometimes the day herder with his band of loose horses was the pathfinder over untracked hills. From year to year as the cattle increased on the range, we built new corrals in hitherto unoccupied territory. The cowboys on such occasions were changed into rather clumsy and inefficient woodsmen and teamsters, the wagons being dispatched to the distant mountains for poles and posts. At other times our work might be delayed for days by rains.

The spring work finished, the different outfits returned to their several headquarters, and the men justified their continuance on the payroll by rendering some assistance in putting up hay. It was an axiom that the cowboy was willing to do anything that could be done on horseback, but was reluctant to do anything else.

On the second night after our return from the spring round-up I had an experience with my herd which at the time was quite exciting. The night was one of the darkest I had ever known; the clouds, dense and heavy, seemed almost within reach of my hand. The keen senses of my horses were my main reliance, although the varied sounds from the herd were full of meaning to me. In the middle of the night I discovered that the herd had moved into the valley of Ford Creek, but whether I was above or below the ranch was quite outside of my knowledge. In the vain hope that I might be able to determine the fact by such inspection as I could give to the stream and its willow-shrouded windings, I groped blindly through the Stygian darkness. While I was engaged at the almost hopeless task at some distance from the herd, two rifle shots in quick succession broke the silence. I could hear the angry whine of the bullets and felt the conviction so common, but almost invariably erroneous, that I had escaped by a narrow margin. My horse leaped beneath me as if stung, and his terror was fully shared by the entire herd, which stampeded out of the valley at a breakneck gallop. Never before was I glad to have my herd stampede.

I encouraged their flight by every silent means, and our headlong pace was continued until we had covered about five miles when, with almost perfect unanimity, to the accompaniment of much snorting and other evidence of equine loquacity, the herd stopped. As to our whereabouts I was only certain that we were away, but I soon found that we were at the pasture gate within fifty yards of the ranch house.

There we stayed until it was time to turn the horses into the little pasture where they would remain until the day herder took them out. My alarm was not unfounded. It developed that my herd had reached the stream in the vicinity of Duffy's place. Duffy had some cherished work horses, and being a prudent man aware of the horse-thief menace, he was in the habit of placing his animals in a padlocked corral at night. Aroused by suspicious sounds, he had discovered two miscreants removing his padlock and had offered remonstrance with his Winchester.

CHAPTER XXVIII

ROBBERS' ROOST

HE BETWEEN round-up season was a lazy time in which colts were broken and much fancy work was done in hair and rawhide. Two men were kept busy in their proper sphere during this interval. Our range was fan-shaped. The home ranch was located at the handle of the fan, and the extended arc of the eastern boundary was the Bad Lands along the Missouri, unsettled and unstocked, the secure retreat of horse thieves and desperadoes, occasionally visited by nomadic Indians. The two range riders devoting five or six days to the trip, left the home ranch and circled the ill-defined easterly limit of our grazing ground. They "traveled light," with one pack horse and few impedimenta. Ordinarily their weekly trip could be viewed as an enjoyable outing. Sometimes they had to report the depredations chargeable to our lawless neighbors, and those outrages against property became more numerous as the secure outlaw retreats along the river became more populous. Steamboat navigation of the Missouri was declining, but there was still some excuse for the woodcutter who supplied fuel for the infrequent boats. The woodyards had become a haven for desperadoes driven out of settled communities east and west, headquarters for criminals of every frontier type.

For their nefarious purposes the location was ideal. The occasional steamboat furnished them with provisions and was not interested in the character of the customer. There were no roads in their vicinity and nothing in the way of casual travel or traffic. Horse stealing became the real business of these communities and was efficiently organized. Horses stolen in British provinces were driven to these retreats and, after some recuperation and alteration of brands, were driven slowly southward in a most innocent manner, to be sold to purchasers in southern Montana or Wyoming. Western horses, in like manner, were disposed of to the farmers of Dakota, while Dakota horses found their market in central and western Montana. The presence and increasing audacity of these marauders had been recognized for a long time. Their depredations, which had at first a coyote character, gradually took on a wolfish aspect. They became emboldened and defiant. No longer confining themselves to thefts in distant territory, they began supplying themselves recklessly and wastefully with beef cattle from our herds and stealing or attempting to steal horses in our immediate vicinity. Owners, following the trail of their stolen horses, prudently dropped the pursuit at the border of the Bad Lands, or failed to return. This picaroon gang was not without its friends and confederates in the turbulent communities where law and order was something more than a pretense. Its members, from the very nature of their nefarious activities, were glad to be advised of matters in which they were interested, such as the departure of an army paymaster with his escort from a northern post to Fort Keogh on the Yellowstone. In this instance a futile attempt was made at a well-selected point to annex the army money. The paymaster traveling in the lead in an ambulance drawn by four mules was commanded to halt by a lurking gang of dismounted desperadoes. Obedience to this audacious summons not being immediate, the driver was shot, whereupon the mules incontinently fled, hauling the paymaster and his treasure box to safety. The infantry escort in an army wagon, following at an absurd distance, was disarmed and allowed to go on its way, its impotence in no wise increased.

In more ways than one this was an unfortunate day for the robber gang. They had slapped Uncle

Sam in the face and that is always unlucky. It was about the third of July 1884, that news came to the home ranch of the presence in our neighborhood of Sam MacKenzie, a half-breed horse thief well known for his reprehensible activities. The horse herd was brought in with a rush, the company carbines and ammunition issued, and we were all in the saddle upon short notice, sent to ride circle for MacKenzie instead of cattle, with instructions, "Go get him!" In riding out, three of us who were sent to a point about ten miles south crossed a trail which we were sure was made by the object of our hunt, but we had been instructed to follow no trail, and reaching the limit of the circle, we scattered and rode back home, scanning the country carefully. Returned to the home ranch we found that MacKenzie had been brought in and was safely deposited in the bunk house with his arms tied behind his back. Three of our men had effected his capture without any attempt at resistance. I satisfied my curiosity as completely as possible without being unmannerly, and I remember this individual quite distinctly. He was dusky, but not dark. In the proper setting his face might be called refined. It had a pallor—which may have been occasioned by his precarious situation—which seemed in keeping with his physiognomy. His bonds were released, and he sat at table with us for the evening meal. At Stuart's house there was serious conclave while we were satisfying our appetites, which had been encouraged by the brisk gallop of the afternoon. MacKenzie was quiet and deferential, displaying little relish for food. One of our parties, returning empty-handed, brought information that they had found two heavily armed, tough-looking characters on a little stream near the IJ horse ranch. So that you may know how to distinguish suspicious characters from others, I can give you Lynn Patterson's account of their behavior: "One fellow didn't have anything to say, but stood behind his horse all the time. The other put on a yellow slicker when he saw us coming, which looked blamed peculiar, for there was no sign of rain, and all the time he talked to us he kept his right hand inside his slicker."

When I took the horses out that night, I was particularly cautioned to be on my guard against any attempt that might be made to run off my herd. These instructions were implicitly obeyed.

Next morning MacKenzie was not there. After the midday meal, I rode with Charley Stuart over to Fort Maginnis, and when we were about half-way to our destination we came upon the mortal remains of Sam MacKenzie dangling from the limb of a cottonwood near the road. In this gruesome sight there was considerable food for reflection.

The incongruities impressed me most. Six feet above the twisted neck and distorted features of the dead horse thief the innocent birds were twittering and flitting about in their leafy shelter. At the base of the tree a bright little stream was placidly gurgling over the clear gravel of its bed. All of the elements of sound and silence proper to a July day were there, and in its midst, terrible yet ludicrous, the pinioned body, swinging and swaying at a rope's end, the center of an admiring concourse of flies.

Either I had some innate idea of the respect due to the dead, or happened on that day to be riding a young horse, but I maintained a deferential distance and indulged in these reflections, while Charley, who was much interested in the beadwork pattern of MacKenzie's moccasins, profited by his curiosity or lack of sensibility by finding, snugly tucked away in one moccasin, a perfectly good silver dollar. We jogged on to the fort, passed the quarters of the married men and civilian employees, splashed through the brook, passed the stables and the parade ground with the cloaked Gatling gun near the flagstaff, and at the post trader's store squandered our treasure trove for candy and peanuts.

· · · · ·

The events following closely upon the lynching of the half-breed were distinctly significant in the development of Montana and in this transition stage of our border civilization. They afford a glimpse of a new page in the record of vigilante activity, and the future student of what may be called the law of the majority, if he becomes acquainted with the facts of the "horse-thief" year, will be provided with material for many fine-drawn distinctions between the vigilante activities in San Francisco, Alder Gulch, Last Chance, and those of the Missouri Bad Lands. In other localities and upon other occasions law-abiding men have been stung into co-operative action to repress an arrogant, lawless minority. In such cases one execution might be sufficient to overawe the criminal element and make it safe for a peaceable man to follow his vocation unafraid. The situation in east central Montana was fundamentally different. Our little scattered settlements contained their proportion of good and bad characters, but the country as a whole was law abiding. We were guided and controlled, not so much by the firm hand of the law, as by tradition and custom. "Bad men" there were, with no permanent abode until some collision provided them with a shallow grave. On the other hand, the robber's roost on the Missouri was a community evil throughout. Their ideals, standards, and aspirations were malign and accursed. The lynching of MacKenzie could do nothing but exasperate a gang of cutthroats which was so defiant and formidable that it send word to one of its victims, "Tell the —— —— that we have his horses and if he wants them to come and get them," a fine piece of bravado indicative of the fact that this cancerous headquarters of crime *must* be cut out by the roots to be cured.

Two of our best men had been sent out in the early morning to observe the motions of the suspicious pair who had been noticed the day before. It is probable that during the last moments of his last evening on earth the half-breed had become voluble and had furnished information to be weighed and checked up against the mass of evidence already in the possession of Granville Stuart and his associates. They had followed the quarry over the mountains to Lewistown, where a grand Fourth of July celebration was beginning. They returned with news of the pair and the opinion that they could be arrested without serious difficulty. The wayfarers who had so aroused our curiosity were known to their companions as Rattlesnake Jake and Longhaired Owens, outlaws each, with rewards for their capture and return to the Black Hills authorities. This precious pair, with Mac-Kenzie, had planned to steal the entire band of horses belonging to the IJ ranch in the Little Snowy Mountains upon the night of July fourth, when, as they rightly conjectured, the ranch employees would be at the jubilation in Lewistown. Our festivals could be counted upon to continue for two or three days, and the roisterers returning home might be expected to waste three or four more days before reaching the conclusion that their horses had been driven away, which would give the thieves a desirable lead.

I presume that upon the morning of the Fourth of July there was nothing to alarm Jake and Owens seriously except the nonappearance of MacKenzie. They mingled with the crowd in the little village and took part in a horse race or two, but their mood changed, and I am inclined to believe that the change resulted upon the receipt of the news, which passed rapidly through the throng, of MacKenzie's fate. Upon the inadequate basis of a trivial quarrel with one of Lewistown's half-breed citizens, they ran amuck. Well mounted, heavily armed, malign and forbidding in appearance, loaded down with cartridges, they rode into Lewistown's only street and commenced shooting right and left. There was a hurried scurrying to cover, or perhaps in fairness to the astonished citizens I should say a hurried search for arms. Not all who sought cover remained in their retreats, and the fusillade was one-sided for only a moment. In that brief interval one man was killed, many windows were shattered, and Main Street was pretty thoroughly "smoked." But that moment over, well-directed shots in reply came from doors, windows, and other shelters. One of the desperadoes fell, dying but defiant, near the tent of an itinerant photographer. His companion, uninjured or comparatively so, with chivalry or bravado worthy of a better cause, returned to his dying companion, dismounted, and died beside him, both men riddled with bullets, but emptying their weapons into the dusty earth when they no longer had the strength to elevate them.

On the evening of this eventful Fourth of July, several of our men who had been sent to Lewistown, presumably to effect the capture of Owens and his venomous partner, returned with the news of the shooting, and about the same time there came to the ranch two grim, determined ranchmen from the upper Yellowstone, who had been following the trail of their little band of horses and had accepted advice and abandoned the trail on the edge of the Bad Lands. Their curiosity satisfied, their indignation only increased, and the conference on the fifth of July resulted in prompt and decisive action.

CHAPTER XXIX

CLEANING THE ROOST

I N THE activities which followed I had little part. I feel quite safe in saying that there was never in the history of America such a thorough, systematic, and successful campaign against outlawry, and I regret my inability to relate with particularity the stirring events which followed each other in such rapid succession during what was ordinarily the lazy vacation period between round-ups. For reasons which at that time did not seem wholly satisfactory, I was left behind, while my comrades to a man, with commendable alacrity, volunteered and were accepted for the dangerous duty of cleaning up the bandits. I was told that it was more important than anything else that our horse herd should be carefully guarded against expected attack. I was the only man left on the ranch; the three Stuart boys shared the duty of day herding the horses, while I continued my work as night hawk, under the admonition to be alert. An endeavor was made, more or less successful, to convince me that my post in the rear was as important and dangerous as any other. I will confess that on the first night after the departure of our formidable party of eighteen men, whatever may have been my opinion of the importance of my position, I was convinced of its danger.

The night, as I recall it, was overcast and dark. I took my well-trained and contented horses to some good grass on a rolling bench north of the ranch and settled down to the humdrum of the night's work. There was an early break in the monotony, when the whole herd, as if in response to an electric shock, stampeded and ran for about a mile before I managed to stop them. The herd once stopped, I rode around them to investigate. I could find nothing suspicious, but there remained much latent uneasiness. The horses had hardly quieted down to grazing before they ran again, and when I succeeded in quieting them, the character of the country showed me that we were three or four miles from home. Fifteen minutes later they found occasion for another fright and took me another mile or so away from home, still nearer the Missouri. By this time I was as panicky as my horses. The mysterious, intangible elements in these little stampedes were most disquieting. If my horses were being driven by mounted robbers, I could have seen the men. If they were being frightened by anyone on foot, the predatory pedestrian would have been left behind in the first run. Finally I resolved upon a countermove. Some action upon my part seemed imperative, and with all the skill at my command, I roused the herd into motion, urging the laggards with my rawhide lasso, and stampeded the herd at a furious gallop back to their original grazing ground. And here, as an anticlimax, I discovered trailing behind the herd a bouncing wooden picket pin at the end of a long rope. No clairvoyance was needed to know that at the other end of the rope there was an outside horse, an unbidden guest, who was the obvious cause of the stampede.

After a quiet day for the depopulated ranch, I took my horses out for another night. When the light of day had entirely disappeared, there was substituted the glow of a young moon among the fleecy clouds. The future reader may consult an ancient almanac and discover that there was no moon on that night and throw my narrative into the discard, but the impression is very distinct that I was easily able to see across the herd with some clearness.

About ten o'clock I saw two horsemen approaching slowly, and I was confident that the time of my test was at hand. Since the day when we rode out in search of MacKenzie I had been carrying my "peacemaker" with a cartridge in each of the six chambers. It was a reliable weapon and I was no novice in its use. I felt abiding confidence in my skill with the six-shooter and the excellence of my eyes. I watched the riders circling the herd, and rode into a depression to meet them, so that I should not be silhouetted against the sky. I remembered, in the midst of some trepidation, that no one excelled me in night craft. The mysterious riders appeared in outline against the sky, and in order that my test might not be delayed, I set spurs to my horse and with my six-shooter in my hand, out of the obscurity of the little valley I dashed upon them with utmost speed. A call of warning and recognition reached me before I felt ready to pull the trigger and I discovered that the mysterious riders were emissaries from the ranch house, sent out to inform me that the expedition had returned. We drove the herd back to the ranch to receive the saddle and pack animals of the returned party as well as the recovered horses belonging to the Yellowstone ranchers. Beyond the fact that all had returned safely, I knew nothing of the result of the foray, until morning.

It may be believed that I was consumed with curiosity, but the seriousness of the matter in hand forbade inquiry. A certain consideration for the natural reticence of my comrades at that time will explain an element of haziness in my relation of those stirring days. I was to learn, however, that their mission was as successful as it was sudden. They left an unmistakable warning in the shape of three lynched outlaws, brought back a band of sixty-five stolen horses, besides a great deal of information, and were accompanied by "Flopping Bill Cantrell," an honest woodcutter who for some years had been leading a lonesome and disgusted existence in the neighborhood of outlawry.

There were a few days of rest after the return, days which on the surface appeared normal, but were in reality the gathering of strength for another blow. In this time I had opportunity to observe Cantrell and another ranch neighbor, who had volunteered to avenge the loss of the cherished horses. Bill was not to be called a centaur, he was an ungainly horseman, much over six feet in height, bony, muscular, slow moving, with a bearing of combined reticence and dignity. I identified him as of Appalachian origin. He was an "Ironside," although I never detected the Bible. The ranchman volunteer was undoubtedly a "singed cat," for he proved himself a natural-born fighter. He was as uncouth as imagination could picture, violating in his garb every known rule of the frontier. He wore shoes when other men wore boots, and his discouraged socks disclosed sunburned shins. He wore suspenders and crowned his sartorial misdemeanors with a straw hat. Under the equivocal brim of this straw hat could be seen a decided Roman nose with its sunburned and peeling surface suggesting the hay field. The nose was flanked by two very bright and alert eyes, and these features, with a quizzical mouth, might have belonged to a man in the company of Drake or Hawkins. He carried no six-shooter, but fondled caressingly a heavy Winchester.

There was little evidence of haste in the preparations for the grand assault. The first blow had been struck before the outlaws had received news of their departed trio, and was directed against what might be called an outpost. The decisive action was perhaps delayed to allow a concentration of the outlaw forces at their general headquarters. At length the sober and steadfast party set out from the ranch in about the same numbers as before. We waited during breathless days and nights. Our anxiety was relieved by the sight of our men coming over the brow of a distant hill, their numbers intact, driving before them a large band, about eighty-five head of recovered horses. Here again my consuming curiosity was stifled, and what I gleaned of the details of the siege of the bandit

The outlaws' hangout on the Missouri.

stronghold must be told, not as historical fact, but as detached items, with a strong admixture of conjecture.

They found, as was hoped and expected, that the outlaws, both stunned and enraged by the Fourth of July misadventure and the audacity of the first foray, had swarmed to their citadel, where they hoped to repel any attack. I retain no picture of their hangout from my Missouri River trip in 1880, but a picture can be pieced together from descriptions which I gathered bit by bit. A level piece of bottom land on the south bank of the Missouri River once heavily timbered with aged cottonwoods, as attested by the remaining stumps and a few scattered logs, and these evidences of an old abandoned wood-yard, once the legitimate purpose of the place, half obliterated by wild growths, clumps of tall rye grass and blooming thickets of the wild rose, all striving to cover the scars of man's outrages. This verdant level was closely flanked by barren Bad Land hills, guttered and carved by the rain of ages. Twenty feet below, the silent river, fringed with willows, flowed rapidly. Not far from the cutbank where the level bottom land breaks off sharply into the seasonal alluvium there was a large log cabin, loopholed for defense, a heavy corral, and a small stable. At some distance from the house, not twenty-five yards from the cutbank, stood a tent, gleaming white in its green setting.

Our party by good management and good fortune were enabled to surround their objective unobserved, before the advent of broad daylight, and waited tense and determined for the coming of the conflict. After a time that seemed interminable, when the July sun was high in the heavens, the door of the cabin opened, and a man, leisurely stretching and yawning, strolled out into the warm sunshine directly toward the station of one of our boys, who, like all others, had been cautioned to wait for the signal shot. The leader, hoping that more of the gang might appear, delayed firing as long as he dared, but finally gave the signal. The course of the sauntering scamp had taken him somewhat out of range, and the echoes of the sharp report had hardly ceased before a ludicrous spectacle obtruded itself upon the tragic stage.

The well-intentioned shot had left the outlaw unharmed, but had torn off the top button of his trousers, which happened to be the only button in service, and the first steps of his flight towards the cabin sanctuary threw him to the ground, hobbled by the fallen garment. His embarrassment was soon ended, for firing became general, especially where three of our men had taken position under the cutbank facing the door of the tent. This tent was the enigma of the attack, and events proved that its importance had been underestimated. To say that the three besiegers peering over their natural breastwork were surprised when the tent emptied itself would be using great reserve in description. In almost immediate response to the commencement of shooting, six men ran out of the tent, fully dressed and fully armed. The numerical inequality was further increased when, at the first shot, one of our three men fainted and rolled down the bank. The two who remained pumped their Winchesters industriously and to some effect, facing a return volley which spattered them with sand and was disconcerting to say the least. The outlaws, however, were in the open and exposed to fire from other quarters, for which they had no stomach, and those who were able soon broke into panic flight for the dense willows along the river.

If these fugitives had retained their morale, the result of the siege might have been quite different. As it was, their presence at large, armed and unhurt, constituted a serious menace, so their flight through dense willows and far away was urged as energetically as possible by heavy firing at random into the sheltering thickets, and soon they were no longer in the battle. The log cabin was responding

spitefully, first from one loophole, then from another, and the attackers, their position disclosed by
the white smoke from their black powder cartridges, were in no little danger when they lifted a
head above stump or log. As the day progressed
shooting became desultory. The heat was truly
oppressive; hardly any of our men were provided
with water, and almost none of them dared leave
shelter. Under the oppression of the twin discomforts, heat and thirst, the day wore on. Before
night a daring attempt to fire the building met
with final success, and when night settled down
the flickering flames of the dying fire lighted the
place of retribution with its lynched outlaws and
exhausted avengers.

It was deemed so vitally necessary that the outlaw band should be completely broken up that an
immediate return to the home ranch was not considered, and the dangerous and difficult task of
tracing and ferreting out the fugitives was commenced on the next day. This work required great
caution, and it was finally agreed that the hunted
men had escaped down the river in some craft of
which they had knowledge. More time than was
expected had been consumed in this expedition and
our party was entirely without provisions. The
robbers' supply had been burned in the cabin. Our
men were in some real extremity when the ap-

proach of a steamboat was noted, coming up the river. Taking a position where a request might be changed to a demand, they hailed the boat, and upon its coming reluctantly to the bank, purchased a supply of provisions. The return home with the encumbrance of the recovered horses was without incident.

Immediately upon the arrival of the party at the DHS ranch, army officers in charge of detachments at points down the river, Poplar River, Fort Peck, and Wolf Point, were notified of the flight of the fugitives. The memory of the attempt upon the paymaster and his escort urged them to efficient action, and through the aid of the recently organized Indian police, the six unhappy wretches were arrested and held under guard. To the direct and unsophisticated mind of our community these men were not only tried and convicted of their crimes, but had clinched the conviction by confession. In spite of this they would be surrendered only to lawful authorities, and a deputy sheriff from Fort Maginnis with a posse selected from our numbers was promptly dispatched to take over the prisoners. It was perhaps ten days that they were gone. During this time there were occasional references to the great effort so successfully concluded, although as might be expected there was reticence —every man who had taken part had been sobered by the awful experience. There was at the same time a noticeable relaxation of tension and a feeling of relief, expressed or concealed by us all. I took the extra cartridge out of my six-shooter and my night work with the augmented herd reverted to its humdrum character.

The recovered horses, about eighty-five in number, were worthy of study and received it. In the band there were horses stolen from Wyoming, from western Montana, from Idaho, and from Dakota, to say nothing of Canadian horses, among them a few with the royal insignia V R burned on the hoof. Some brands had been effaced more or less successfully; others had been changed or were in process of change, and it was a difficult task to discover ownership.

At length the sheriff's posse returned empty-handed, with some fishy explanation that a masked party had surprised them at night and taken their prisoners from them. The story was unsatisfactory, but sufficient to check inquiry as to details. Somewhat later a traveler told us of a gruesome sight seen near the mouth of the Musselshell—nine bodies hanging from the cottonwoods.

As the story of this critical period is being told by me for the first time in many years, I am conscious of two things: that after these years of silence

UBET

I find that my memory is reluctant, possibly unreliable as to details, and that the bald narrative reviewed in the security and quiet of these days has a quality of brutality and unnecessary inhumanity altogether outside our convictions and standards of 1884. I feel certain that not one man who took part in the terrible task of cleaning up the outlaws was animated or influenced by any motive lower than the desire to restore security and order, and that every act necessary to the accomplishment of the task was looked upon as a death grapple between the honest men of the community and crime, arrogant and entrenched. It will be asked, "Why were the forms of law ignored? Why, for instance, should Sam MacKenzie be deprived of his life when he was found doing nothing more criminal than jogging his saddle horse across vacant country on a hot July afternoon?" The answer to this question is that through repeated experience we of the frontier had found that the voice of the law could be heard, but that her protecting arm could not reach us.

Respectable citizens, safe in their home and property, will perhaps notice that to this day if a suspected criminal barricades himself in his den, he comes forth a corpse, denied all protection which the law draws about the man accused. The ruffians who retreated to the block-house after the first skirmish, by the very act admitted their guilt and complicity in the crimes of which their evil association boasted.

As to the men who took upon themselves the duties of judge, juror, and executioner, I can say that their leader, Granville Stuart, exceptional for education, experience, wisdom, and patience, honored in later years by the office of Ambassador to Uruguay, and my comrades and the ranchmen who volunteered for the desperately dangerous work have, without exception, in their later lives *proved* that they were no raffish swashbucklers. My chum, the flute player, who was reading John Stuart Mill that summer, was later an honored and respected judge on the Pacific Coast. How often, as he decides the causes brought before him, must he recall the part he took in the administration of the rude justice of the frontier.

CHAPTER XXX

I ENGAGE IN
THE CATTLE BUSINESS

IN THE fall when I returned to Ubet I found that my father, anticipating the coming change in the method of handling cattle and also in anticipation of my twenty-first birthday had made some sort of filing upon land up the valley from our home and had erected a large cow barn and had contracted with some Iowa cattle men for one hundred long yearling heifers to be handled by us on shares.

In due time the heifers, or so many of them as remained after a railroad wreck en route, were unloaded at Billings and were driven over the hundred-mile distance by Julius Carter and myself. This was a modern trail herd easily distinguishable from the others in which I had taken part. We had no horses other than the ones we rode. We corralled the cattle at night at ranches or stage stations, and as they were somewhat thin and discouraged, we fed a little hay every day. These cattle were real "dogies," and on this trip I first heard that term used.

I Engage in the Cattle Business

With the new cattle and our own little herd, descended from the aristocrats of 1879, we had quite a respectable bunch of ranch cattle, and what with my work in their management and my services in the post office and stage station, I put in a busy winter.

There were long evenings, however, with no duties beyond those concerned with feeding firewood into our big stove in the saloon, when there was time for education, recreation, and work in preparation for the coming summer. We subscribed for several good magazines and two daily papers, and I spent much time in reading.

I made two or three quirts or cowboy riding whips and commenced a rawhide lariat. I was soaking the strands for their second stretching and it was likely that the odor from the operation reminded "Lying Babcock" of a story. He asked the general company if we had ever heard how Dave Hilger broke his leg. We had not; even the fact itself was doubted, but "Bab" proceeded.

"In the spring of '81 Dave Hilger started from his ranch down near the Moccasins somewhere to go back to his old home in the Missouri Valley. But he had some trouble in getting started. During the winter the coyotes had chewed up all of his harness except the hames and the buckles, and the whole gear had to be patched up with rawhide.

He made four beautiful tugs out of green buffalo hide. They were wide and thick and long and strong, and everything was fine as frog's hair until he got pretty close to Martinsdale. He raised the hill west of Daisy Dean and Frank Gaugler's place was in sight, not more than three miles away, when it commenced to rain to beat all get out. It was one of those warm wet rains, but Dave put on his slicker and climbed out of the overflowing wagon seat to plod along at the head of his nigh horse.

"In about an hour he had reached the place and tied his team to the hitching post, but he nearly fell dead when he found that the wagon was nowhere in sight! His tugs were tight and he knew at once what had happened. The rawhide had stretched! The tugs had been made from a heavy, well-furred piece of hide; now they were no bigger than a lead pencil and the hairs were about two inches apart. Well, Dave started back in the rain to hunt for that wagon. He had followed the tugs for about a mile, when the storm broke and the sun came out with a fresh, drying wind. He started to take off his slicker and that blamed stiff-tongued wagon came up and ran over him.

"The Lord only knows how long he might have lain there, but about that time me and 'Whiskey Myers' stepped out of Frank's place and saw the first horseless carriage in the Territory. It was coming along about as fast as a horse could run, bouncing from side to side and throwing mud twenty feet high. We saw the horses tied to the post standing perfectly still and pulling to beat anything we ever saw. We were speechless and helpless until the wagon stopped exactly where it belonged, with the end of the tongue poked right through the ring in the neckyoke.

"We went down the road and found Dave, and I took him in his own rig up to Doc Parberry at the Springs, but you bet if it had started to rain, I would have gone into camp right there."

The winter passed as winters have a habit of doing. There was much carrying in of wood and carrying out of ashes. It was planned that I should forsake my cowboy vocation and devote myself to the care of our growing ranch herd. I filed upon my claim, which now in addition to the large barn had a small house, which was technically my home. The time for joining the round-up passed and I was fairly committed to the new program, when a cattleman friend asked me to go to Washington Territory where he was purchasing stock for shipment to Montana. There was hurried consultation in which my inclinations were consulted and we started for the railroad, and the railroad carried us to the western headquarters of the expedition, which was a little station called Lind, somewhere between Ritzville and the Columbia River. We were not mounted but had opportunities to visit some nearby ranches.

One night with a companion I was entertained at a ranch where the head of the house was a giant of a man and he had four sons, almost as large as their father, who ranged from eighteen to twenty-four years of age. There was a good deal of what we called "beef" in that family.

In the course of the evening my companion jokingly asked the old man for a job as broncho buster, but there was no opening. My companion then wanted to know how they handled their colts. "Oh," said the old man, that's easy. We get a colt in the corral and I get a rope on him and then every child grabs a leg." My mental picture of an overmatched broncho vainly struggling in the hands of these sons of Anak was so vivid that the rallying cry, "Every child grab a leg," has become a family heritage.

The country in that section of Washington impressed me as unsettled, but tame. It was open grass land, with occasional basaltic hills. The soil was the lightest sand I ever saw; if a horse stepped within a foot of a badger hole he would break through, and horse and rider would go down in a column of dust, but no casualties resulted. The infrequent ranchmen seemed to have everything but money. They had fat horses and cattle, pigs, sheep, and chickens, and wonderful fruit, but no market.

There were several trainloads of cattle, and in the course of time my train of cattle was loaded and we started east. The railroad had been in operation as a through line for about two years. The motive power on the western division consisted, insofar as freight traffic was concerned, of small wood-burning Baldwin locomotives. We had great difficulty in pulling some of the hills. Every member of the train crew believed that the trouble would be done away with if the newly installed speed-clock in the caboose should get out of order. The officials on their high stools at division headquarters were very prompt to reprimand a crew guilty of making any speed in excess of twenty miles an hour. This ruling gave them no chance to take a run at a hill. On one of our trains, John Smith, the foreman, made himself popular by destroying the recording mechanism of the caboose clock by "accidentally" discharging his six-shooter.

I had one harrowing experience on this trip. Our train was laboring through the Bitter Root Mountains and there was an immense country within view. In order that I might see as much as possible I climbed to the top of the cars and walked from car to car towards the head of the train. There was one car in that section of the train that was out of repair, the diagonal bracing at the front being broken. I stepped upon this car and was walking rapidly forward, when I found myself staggering in a most absurd manner upon a footing that was shaking like jelly. I escaped a fall by dropping to my hands and knees and clinging to the running board. Tragically, for my peace of mind, the train at this time was crossing Marent Gulch on the highest wooden trestle in the world, two hundred and twenty-six feet! The crossing was made very slowly, and my precarious chariot did not shake so alarmingly, but I was very happy when I was safely across that awful chasm.

Our cattle, one trainload after another, were unloaded at Townsend, Montana. We moved them up the river a few miles, then camped for a couple of days while we assembled a trail outfit. We purchased a nondescript lot of horses from neighboring ranchers and hired enough men and boys to handle the herd on the trail. There were four men in our party who could be called cowboys. We had six or seven others who were not even entitled to the appellation by courtesy. This explains our boss's request that Ray and I, night herders, should rope and doctor a steer that had broken one horn during the railroad journey and was pestered with blow-flies.

I Engage in the Cattle Business

Accordingly we saddled up and rode out to the herd after breakfast, where Ray, with commendable dexterity, caught the steer at the first throw. Ray was riding for the occasion a runaway buggy horse, with a makeshift bridle and snaffle bit, his proper equipment having been looted during our absence in Washington. The throwing of the rope was the signal for a spirited runaway, the steer going south, while Ray and his charger headed for the Arctic Circle, leaving a faint odor of burnt leather from the saddle horn. This was my opportunity, and, after a few skillful maneuvers, I duplicated Ray's clever work in its entirety, and departed in a great hurry for Three Forks, leaving the steer somewhat astonished and perplexed, trailing two perfectly good lassos through the interested herd.

In the course of time, Ray returned from his Arctic expedition and we tried in vain to recover the loose ends of our ropes. At every attempt to reach the ground, our horses promptly bolted. We then borrowed ropes from the two men on herd, and Ray made a second attempt, which resulted in another runaway. The steer, now decorated with his third rope, trotted sulkily in one direction, while Ray's horse in a runaway frenzy dashed into the herd. Many of the cattle were lying down, and the horse plunged among the astonished animals without seeking a clear pathway. I saw him headed directly for a recumbent cow. I saw Ray pull his feet from the stirrups and place both hands on the horn with an outburst of profanity perfectly justifiable in view of the inevitable collision. The frantic horse struck the half-aroused cow as she was rising in leisurely bovine fashion, and Ray, like an erratic projectile, was catapulted through the sagebrush and cactus for an incredible distance, sustained in his flight by a flow of objurgatory language I have never heard equalled.

In the course of time and after many efforts, the injured steer was treated with the proper medicaments and Ray and I returned to camp for our afternoon sleep, fully convinced that education was required of a cow-horse, as well as of a cow-man.

The next day we started the herd into the mountains on its way to its new home. We drove them down the south fork of the Musselshell and into the Judith Basin, where they were turned loose.

I saw Ray pull his feet from the stirrups and plant both hands on the horn.

CHAPTER XXXI

TRAILING THE BEEF
TO THE RAILROAD

LATE in the fall I looked for an opportunity to go back to the states with cattle and accepted with some reluctance a night herding job, for the drive to the railroad. Night herding in June, July, or August is quite different from the same job in October. It is probable that the Fates knew that this was to be my last contact with range cattle and took pains to give me experience in every kind of misery known to cowboys, except heat. We had a little herd of six hundred beef cattle, well disciplined by their spring experience, for they were part of the herd we had brought through from Washington. We had a stampede the first night on herd, but the cattle did not scatter nor run very far, in spite of the antics of my side-partner, who was a conscientious and trustworthy ranch hand with little cowboy experience. He was handicapped by a pair of poor night eyes, often complaining to me that on a dark night he couldn't see anything but haystacks and corrals, which I could assure him were optical illusions.

We started out with a two-inch fall of snow, which disappeared when we got into the Mussel-shell Valley, but the sky was much overcast and at least twelve of the twenty-four hours were dark. Our night shift instead of being eight hours long, as it ordinarily was in June, was prolonged to eleven hours or worse.

My partner and I used to eat our breakfasts in the dim light of dawn, catch up and picket a saddle horse apiece, and lie down on our saddle blankets with our coats and slickers for covering, to get our quota of sleep while the herd moved on. We were usually stirring by one o'clock; one of us would saddle the horses while the other built a brisk little fire. Into the coals we would throw two thick slices of dry salt pork, to be fished out on a pointed stick a moment later and placed between two slabs of Dutch-oven bread. This primitive hot dog sandwich was our noon meal, after which we followed the trail of the mess wagon to the night camp.

The last portion of our drive was through an unsettled section where we had no road to follow. The weather although not cold was disheartening. One night when a storm seemed imminent there was some discussion between me and my partner as to the proper dress for the occasion. I thought that a cloth overcoat and slicker would be *de rigeur,* while he favored a buffalo coat. About midnight it began to rain gently and it continued until we were relieved in the morning. Between our herd and camp there was a guttered little wash about six feet deep and ten feet across, cut through the 'dobe clay. My horse hesitated at the brink, and I could hardly blame him, so I used moral suasion and flattery to overcome his reluctance and at last he sat down and slid to the bottom of the ditch, then clambered out, literally on his hands and knees. I waited for my partner, who had lost his temper and was fighting his horse. He was in a sad plight after the long rain. He was a super-saturated, disintegrating mass. When he swung his quirt he sprayed water from his sleeves and both horse and rider were approaching insanity. Finally he dismounted and to my surprise was sufficiently articulated to stand erect. He tried to lead his horse by the bridle rein, but slipped in the greasy mud and slid to the bottom of the ditch, only to be drawn out again by the frightened horse. He made another attempt with the same result, and each descent into the gumbo added appreciably to his accumulation of mud. On the third trial the bridle reins broke, and the riderless horse trotted off to the horse herd. It was quite impossible for my partner to climb the steep bank of the ravine without assistance, so I took down my rope and tossed one end to him and hauled him out by the horn of my saddle. Without this help he might have been a total loss. As it was, the gross weight of the saturated aggregate must have been near three hundred pounds, of man, buffalo coat, and mud.

After a hearty breakfast my partner, somewhat reconditioned, lay down beside me in the damp grass to get a measure of sleep while the herd and the mess outfit went on their way. The sky was overcast, but the air was warm, and we slept soundly. When we waked up I looked at my cheap watch and noted with some surprise that it was only a quarter past twelve. We were pleased to feel so much refreshed by such a short rest. While we were toasting our bacon, it began to snow in a hesitating manner, and we hurried our departure. Looking at my watch again I found that it had stopped, and in the absence of sun, the real time was a matter of mere conjecture. Snow was falling more persistently, and it seemed to be growing dark. We followed the track made by the wagon wheels, but noted with some disquiet that the increasing snow made the process more difficult. We found that the tracks were only discernible where the wagon had crossed some depression, leaving a plain trail in the rank grass. Then came the time when the trail was completely lost and we had in prospect a camp for the night without food or bedding, a situation that only required a drop in temperature to become very serious. We were in consultation about our predicament, when we heard a most welcome sound—far away someone was using an axe, and toward that sound we rode as rapidly as possible. When it stopped we went into a huddle for an unorthodox but fervent prayer. At last we reached port; it was not a camp in the proper sense, for our mess wagon had broken a reach in an attempt to scale an escarpment, and all of our duffle had been dumped to facilitate road-side repairs. Somewhere out in the hills, in a smother of snow, was the herd and six hungry cow-boys. We worked for about half an hour in an endeavor to keep moving, but finally gave up and put up a tent after a fashion.

I rode to the top of the hill and fired a few rounds from my six-shooter, but got no response. We could pretty well conjecture what was happening with the beef herd, but we slept and wakened in the morning to find that the warmth of the ground had melted much of the snow, and after breakfast, my partner and I, each leading a spare horse and carrying good-sized lunches for our hungry comrades, started our search for the missing cattle. We separated, so as to cover as much territory as possible, and rode into a rough, uninhabited section where it was exceedingly difficult to lay out or maintain a course on account of heavy, low-hanging clouds with which the land was blanketed. All hilltops were cut off by the clouds, which were so low that they seemed within reach of one's hand.

I had not ridden far until, without warning, I came upon a band of twelve large wolves! I was within fifty yards of the pack before I discovered them. They seemed to have no important business on hand, and for the moment I forgot my errand and watched them. They were big, prosperous-looking fellows, who stared at me with frank curiosity; if there was any timidity, I am sure I contributed my share. I put the sixth cartridge in my Colt's and wondered whether I should have time to reload. I found myself in a tender-hearted mood and was pleased when the pack sauntered away with hardly a glance over their shoulders.

I rode for miles, but could find no trace of the herd. I saw but one man, a Scandinavian sheepherder, who gave me a great deal of information in a language totally unintelligible. As the afternoon was waning, I followed down the course of a little rivulet, knowing that all drainage in the locality must reach the Yellowstone, and at dusk I came up with six very lank cowboys, all with gaunt, leg-weary horses, who had just placed their cattle in the stockyards and were headed toward a section house for their first meal in thirty hours. We had mountain trout for supper; my comrades could rest while they ate, but were too busy to comment on their own experiences, so I told them of the plight of the mess wagon and we went to our makeshift beds.

There was some trouble about getting cars at this isolated shipping point, so we boys boarded with the section man, and his good wife gave us trout for breakfast, dinner, and supper, and again for breakfast. We expected to get loaded before noon, but were somewhat delayed, and I was sent back to the section house about eleven o'clock to ask if we could get a noonday meal. The good woman glanced at the kitchen clock and announced her willingness, adding, "I must hurry and get some fish." She took a fishpole standing near the front door and hurried to the bank of the river, much more certain that she would get her fish than is the housewife of today who goes marketing, and—we had fish for dinner.

CHAPTER XXXII

MORE YARNS

OUR RAILROAD journey east was started in a mixed train. There were two double-decked carloads of wethers just ahead of the caboose, and the owner of the wethers, a large, good-natured, round-faced man, was the fourth member of our caboose group. There was at that time considerable ill-feeling between cowboys and sheepmen, but this old fellow was a real character, and by the time our train reached Glendive, about midnight, complete harmony prevailed.

We unloaded our cattle very expeditiously upon arrival, and, to show the completeness of the newly established brotherhood, we delayed our departure from the yards until the sheepman got his cars emptied. He had the car door open and was in the chute trying to unload the lower deck first, which as we found was faulty technic, he should have begun operations with the upper deck. His success was not noticeable. One of our boys was on the off side of the car, using his prod pole and objectionable language, but getting precisely nowhere.

The sheepman set his lantern down and almost on all fours entered the lower deck. He grabbed a wether and hauled him forth. When the struggling pair were out of the car, trouble began, for the sheep in the upper deck began their exit. The first one landed on the old man, flattening him out quite completely. He was followed by a Niagara of bleating "woollies" and while it is hardly possible that *all* of them jumped on the prostrate owner, his ruin was almost complete. His lantern was broken and extinguished, his clothing was torn, and he retired bleeding and bruised.

We knew nothing about sheep and were proud of it, but we unloaded the other car without trouble and went to our lodgings. About thirty hours later we were again rolling eastward. There was a new make-up to our train, which now consisted of cattle only.

The day was of a sort to be remembered. The autumn air was clear and crisp. The sunshine was bright and filled our world with a chaste warmth. A moderate westerly gale pursued us, and the smoke from the locomotive at times preceded us and at other times when we were moving at equal speed, a black column from our smokestack ascended to great heights, a pillar of smoke by day. The caboose was no place for me in such weather, and I went over the top of the cars to make the acquaintance of the head brakeman. We sat on the sunny side of the car with our feet dangling over its narrow eaves and talked of many things. I found that he was a graduate of the cow camp and had been railroading for about three years. When I told him of our recent adventures, he recounted his last cowboy experience, which I deem worthy of insertion, showing as it does the militant democracy of the old West and the cowboy's loyalty to his outfit.

"Five years ago I was coming north with a small trail herd. Our old man was kind of a Texas Yankee, and when we struck the U. P. he split the herd and sold the beef to some Chicago buyers and he got a good price for the she stuff from a tenderfoot by the name of Eastman, who was the son of a First National Bank, or something of that sort, back east. He was a good-looking young fellow, as pink and clean as a link of fresh pork sausage, but he had been horribly mishandled in the way of clothes. He wore little short panties made out of corduroy with heavy wool stockings and high shoes. He had a corduroy coat with kind of tucks in it, so that if he swelled up he wouldn't bust it. He had a broad-brimmed hat, but it wasn't a sombrero; I reckon you could call it a mushy flop. He was armed to the teeth with a big bowie knife and a .32 caliber aggravation, and it was hung on the wrong side in a holster with a lovely flap, so that if he wanted his gun in a hurry, he would have to get a button hook or a can opener to get at it. But he was a nice fellow; I liked him from the start.

"When the steers were cut out, the outfit split up, and Don Rutherford, the foreman, me and four other fellows, and the cook and the mess wagon were to go north to young Eastman's ranch on Gray Bull. Don was a Texan, except he wasn't born there. His folks lived in Tennessee somewhere, but they planned to go to Texas as soon as they could, and when Don was born they thought it would be real romantic to give him a Spanish name, so they called him 'Don Carlos.' When they got to Texas and found how ornery and trifling the greasers were, it was too late to change his name. He was a *real* man and understood his business. I allow he was about twenty-five years old and the homeliest fellow I ever saw. He had a face like a platter of cold meat and it hadn't been improved any by a big scar across his cheek and nose.

"We started out short of almost everything, especially tobacco. It seemed as though everybody got short at the same time, so when we were pretty close to the railroad, Eastman took the cook and wagon and struck out for a little town ten or twelve miles west, for supplies. We went on with only a loaf of bread or so and some cold meat for our noon meal. The outfit was to be back that night.

"That was a miserable day. It was getting along in the fall, and the whole country was as dry as a lime burner's wig and the wind blew great guns. We found water for the cattle at noon, then drifted them north towards some rim rock buttes which had been pointed out as the night camp. When night came there was no mess outfit, no bedding, no grub, and no tobacco! We night-herded in three reliefs and kept a big fire burning to keep ourselves warm and to guide the outfit to camp in case they were lost, but nothing showed up.

"Next morning we had a kind of a council of war, but Don wouldn't listen to anything except to keep moving. None of us knew the country, but our general direction had been pointed out towards a mountain range way off, and Don said it was our business to keep the cattle moving. The wind came up with the sun and blew so blamed hard it blew the ears off some of the horses. Whenever we got a chance someone would ride to the top of a butte to see if the outfit was in sight, but all day long we were alone with the wind and the alkali dust. There was no sign of a settler, and I don't wonder at it;

the Creator was certainly darned slack when He made Wyoming.

"At noon we camped on a little creek at least three inches wide and about the color of good tea. We killed a calf that day, but it wasn't a calf that belonged to the herd; it was a maverick we had picked up two days before. That will show you how thrifty Rutherford was. There wasn't much meat left when we got through, but we took what there was and wrapped it in the hide to keep some of the dust out and away we went. We drove about six miles that afternoon and made a dry camp. Still no outfit was in sight. There was a little puddle of water, about a barrelful in a ravine, the puddle was full of bird feathers and didn't taste exactly right, but we had burned veal to eat and that water to drink that night and next morning.

"We couldn't make out why the mess outfit didn't show up, we knew that the cook would get drunk if he had a chance, but Eastman was along and had a saddle horse and the team was steady and reliable, so we gave up thinking and smoked cigarettes made of dry grass and buffalo chips. I don't recommend them!

"Next morning when no outfit was in sight, some of the boys were ready to quit, but Don laid down the law to them and nothing more was said about it. So we plugged along with the wind blowing harder, I believe, than it did the day before. By pure good luck we managed to strike water for the cattle about noon, and in the afternoon we followed the creek pretty close, as it was in line with our general direction, but we didn't see a ranch nor a human being—not even a claim shanty—all that day.

"Don promised us that if we ever found a decent camp, he would kill another calf and we would lay over and send a man back to the railroad to see what had fetched loose with the outfit. But late that afternoon a fellow came riding down off the bench (how he found us I don't know, for we hadn't seen him); at first we thought it was Eastman, but it wasn't, although he was dressed pretty much like him. He was a little fellow with glasses, the tenderest kind of a tenderfoot. The first thing Don asked him was whether he had any tobacco, but he said no, he didn't smoke, and Don said, 'Well you might have brought us some.' 'Mr. Eastman forgot to get any,' said Curlylocks. After telling us that they had made camp about a mile up the creek, he rode away.

"When we saw the camp we got the cattle out of the creek bottom onto a high, dry bench and left the fattest man to hold them, because we thought he would last longer than the rest of us, and then we just burnt the earth getting into camp. We didn't stop to unsaddle, we just swarmed around the fire. Then we saw that our old cook had been lost in the shuffle and there was a Chinaman at work.

"The little fellow with the glasses was sitting on the ground with his back against a tree, and there was another fellow dressed just like him alongside, but we were not interested in tenderfeet. Don made a flying jump for the messkit, got his equipment, and speared a boiled potato. When he straightened up, Eastman said to him in the most matter-of-fact way, 'Boys, you will have to wait until these gentlemen eat.' Nobody said anything for a minute, except my partner, he said, 'Like Hell we will!' But I was watching Don, I couldn't do anything else. I was like a chicken looking at a chalk mark and he was worth looking at. His hat was tilted back, and all around his forehead little tight curls of his black hair were glued with sweat and alkali dust. His eyebrows were dusted white, he had a four-day beard that was plumb saturated with dust and gravel, and a good deal of it had been glued in with blood and grease from our fatted calf. His face was almost as black as a nigger's, except for that scar; it seemed that dirt wouldn't stick to that. He had a lot of creases around his eyes and they looked pink and wet, but the edges of them were pure mud. He was something awful to look at.

"After a minute Don spoke up in a kind of soft and pleading way. He said, 'Mr. Eastman, I *do* want to be reasonable, so if you will kindly listen to me I will tell you why I think I ought to eat without any delay. In the first place I am a better man than you are—I want you to say yes to that.' By golly, I don't blame Eastman for saying yes to that. 'I come from a better family than you do. Speak up and say yes to that,' he said. 'I am better educated than you.' 'Yes,' said Eastman. 'I am hungrier than you are—I have been taking care of your cattle and living like a coyote while you were playing croquet at the railroad, and besides, I am cleaner and sweeter and better-looking than you are. Now you take your hoop and run away and play somewhere, and when we get through, if there is anything left, you and those two pink warts can eat.' And all this time he was waving his fork and a great big boiled potato right under Eastman's nose. It was a sight to look at.

"Eastman was first pink and then pale. His mouth was twitching and he was kind of watery about the eyes. He walked away and we tackled our dinner. I never ate so much in my life. When we were through, Eastman came back looking kind of funny. He walked up to Rutherford and looked him right square in the eye (I always did like that youngster) and said, 'Mr. Rutherford, I want to apologize to you.' Don's face softened as much as it could under the dirt. 'I was an inconsiderate damn fool,' says Eastman, 'and I am ashamed of myself, but I gave my assent to one proposition which I wish to retract.' Don's face didn't look so soft. 'I agreed that you were clean and sweet and good looking, that is not the truth, you are the homeliest and dirtiest man I ever saw.' Don put out his hand and they shook. 'Perhaps you are right,' he said, 'I could forgive everything if you hadn't forgotten the tobacco.'

"The Chinaman had been running his arm into his war sack, it was one of those matting affairs you have seen Chinamen carry, and he steps up with a big sack of tobacco and a grin clear across his face! Do you know what we did? Well, we just took that old fraud Hayes and kicked him out of the White House and elected that Chinaman President of the United States."

CHAPTER XXXIII

HONESTY IS THE BEST POLICY

ITHIN six weeks after my departure from Ubet on the beef drive, I was at home again to find that my father, who had been ailing all summer, had failed noticeably. About the middle of December he suffered a stroke of partial paralysis, and ten days later he died. He was a good father and a good husband, a man with a mentality above the average, enterprising and forward looking. Had he lived he might have been one of Montana's most valuable citizens. Life went on without him, with much of the burden shifted to the shoulders of my mother and myself.

Real winter, in spite of the threatenings in October, did not come until the New Year arrived. During the summer, our Carter herd had been brought up to one hundred head, and in January and February we were compelled to feed a great deal of hay, as the Iowa members of our herd were not good rustlers. I think it was some time in March that we purchased hay from a neighbor who lived three or four miles away and drove our cattle there to feed from the stack. When the hay had been consumed, the cattle were returned to Ubet, where we continued to feed a small ration, while we waited for spring and new grass.

Two or three days after the cattle had returned home, our neighbor came in for his mail and reported that one of our "dogie" heifers was at his place and was down. We went over there with a team and a low sled and by main strength loaded the discouraged heifer upon the sled, hauled her home and into the stable and managed to get her into one of the stalls. The weather was not cold, but was unpleasant and sloppy, and it was evident that the animal required attention if she was to be saved. I rigged a sling with two *cinchas* and some other gear and hoisted her to her feet for a time, while I rubbed her legs, gave her warm water to drink, and generally gave her the best nursing at my command. Every two or three hours we hoisted her to her feet, and were gratified to note that she began to take an interest in life. One morning she announced her intention to become a mother. This was an unexpected complication, but we were not daunted. Stockmen of experience will know what was done, others will conjecture, but our herd was increased by one small calf who was compelled to take his nourishment from a foster mother for a few days until his own mother was in condition to nourish him. When the cow and calf were discharged from our improvised hospital and went out on the sunny hillside to enjoy the delights of spring weather and good grass, I dismissed them from my mind.

We branded in May. There were very few range cattle in our neighborhood and supposedly none in the Ubet Valley. When the branding day came, I happened to be very busy about post office, stage, and express business and did not once go near the corral. A young cowboy from the Musselshell happened to be at the place and he and my twelve-year-old brother did the roping. Four or five days after the branding, Mr. Morrison from the Judith came to Ubet in great indignation and asked me to look at the cause of his grief. He showed me the young cow that I had saved from an untimely death, with his brand on her left ribs. I never saw a plainer brand, it could be read a quarter of a mile away, and there was the calf, in whom I felt an interest almost fatherly, bearing my fresh brand.

Morrison departed muttering, and I went back to my work cursing! This is but another instance showing that honesty is the best policy.

CHAPTER XXXIV

UBET AGAIN

ET ME describe Ubet as it would appear to an observant traveler, making the stage journey from Billings to Fort Benton in 1886. In the crisp air of early morning the four-horse Concord stage reaches a point where the little settlement can be seen, less than half a mile away. The road enters the place from the east. At the left there are the stage stables, and just beyond them the capacious barn, both being substantial frame buildings. At the right, at some distance from the road, is the blacksmith shop. About opposite the stage stable on the north side of what might be called Main Street, is the post office, stage and express office, both in a building originally intended for a store. Beyond it is the saloon, next to that the ice-house, and last, diagonally opposite the barn, is the Ubet Hotel. The mail sacks are thrown out, the express matter for the local office or for transfer to other lines is unloaded, the male passengers go to the saloon, which under our management was the local club, the stage driver turns over his horses to the stock-tender and, with the dust of travel removed, almost everybody in the hamlet proceeds to the hotel dining room.

Inasmuch as the Ubet dining room was the very heart of Ubet, the prime source of its profit and its title to fame, it deserves description. It was a well-lighted room in the southeast corner of the house, about twenty-two by eighteen feet. It had a spotless, well-scrubbed pine floor. Walls and ceilings were covered with select lumber, painted apple green. Along the north side of the room there was a well-built sideboard with drawers and tilts, and on the wall there hung a very reliable Seth Thomas calendar clock. Two well-mounted deer heads, one a black-tail, the other a white-tail, faced each other from opposite ends of the room and between the windows on the south wall there hung, well framed, a group of photographs of the Wisconsin Assembly of which father had been the speaker. A long table, with spotless white tablecloth and napkins, carried the family silver, supplemented where necessary by a superior quality of plated ware, and the table was supplied with the best food that we could obtain, prepared under my mother's constant supervision. This description may sound commonplace, but in those days of which I write, it was so *very* exceptional, that travelers arranged their schedules so that they might eat at Ubet. It was no longer necessary for a traveler to carry his roll of blankets. We had bedrooms to accommodate ordinary traffic and extra bedding to take care of any overflow.

At the west end of the house was the parlor and "bridal chamber." Both rooms had floor coverings of ingrain carpet, the walls were ceiled with lumber as was the whole house, the space between the ceiling and outer walls being filled with sawdust for warmth. There were several pieces of horsehair covered furniture in the parlor, and the bedroom had an expensive walnut bedroom set, with marble-topped bureau and washstand and an excellent spring mattress. We could offer good food and service and a degree of comfort very rare at that time in the Territory of Montana.

Everybody in the hamlet ate at the hotel, which meant that in addition to our own family and those who assisted us in the management of the place we had the blacksmith, the stock-tender, and the four stage drivers, so that even on dull days, we had a goodly company.

It was discovered after experiments extending over many years, that Ubet was not a good location for merchandising. At the time of my father's death we made no pretense of carrying a stock of goods for sale except wet goods, and our management of the saloon business was peculiar to our place. We had no love for the business of selling whisky, but after one experience in leasing that part of our establishment, we managed it ourselves, so that we might in a measure control it, for Ubet was our home. We thought too highly of our women folk, including the intelligent and self-respecting girls who assisted us in the hotel, to permit any rowdyism. At the forks of the Musselshell the saloon was so full of bullet holes that it was not weatherproof. At Ubet there was one hole in the floor, due to the accidental discharge of a revolver.

In those early days the people of eastern Montana would have been characterized as irreligious, but whenever we were visited by an itinerant missionary, we gave him something more than a respectful hearing. One evening the stage from the west brought beloved Bishop Brewer, en route for Lewistown, and that night he conducted services in our parlor. There were ten or twelve men in the saloon, a serious poker game was in progress and billiard balls were clicking, but when the hour of divine service came, cues were put up, the poker players left their cards and chips on the table, and we all trooped up to the hotel, after locking the saloon doors. After the sermon, when the normal activities of the place were resumed, a group about the stove listened to dog stories. When the subject had been quite well developed by lovers of the dog, Hank Platt said:

"I suppose everything has its place, and I reckon a dog's place is with some crazy sheepherder. That gives the sheepherder a chance to associate with a superior intelligence. The trouble with a dog is that he either knows too much or too little. You've heard me talk about Calvin Stevens? Well, he is a good example of what trouble a dog can make for a man. Just after he moved over from the Musselshell, a fellow came along to his place and stayed over night and then went on his way rejoicing—he had sawed off a dog on Cal. It was a kind of hound dog with long flabby ears 'bout as thick as a buckwheat cake, a spotted dog, black and buckskin and some white. Cal thought it was a very remarkable dog, and he *was* remarkable for two things: he had a wonderful voice (they called him Bugler) and he had a tongue that was about eleven and a half inches long when it was moist— and it was always moist. Of course he was affectionate, you needed a slicker if you didn't make that dog keep his distance. He would slobber all over you, and if you would drive him away, he would go and lick the doorknob for an hour at a stretch; perfectly worthless I'd call him, but Cal and his wife acted as though they had filled a flush. I used to be around Cal's place a good deal and the talk used to be really worth while. Mrs. Stevens was smart as a whip and she had been educated too and we would talk about the Centennial and the war and the blue glass cure and the books we were reading and everything.

"But after Cal got that hound it seemed as though the family intellect was headed south. The dog would lie down on the bearskin rug in the middle of the floor and we would sit around all evening and our talk couldn't be pried loose from that cur. Mrs. Stevens would say, 'See him open his eye,' and then Cal would say, 'Now he's after a flea. Get him Bugler.' Even when the dog was asleep they would sit there and wait for him to snore or something.

"That dog had made a complete mash, but they got cured after a while. The first jolt they got was one day when little Samuel Tilden Stevens (he was about three then) was walking across the creek on the foot-log. Bugler had important business on the other side and knocked the kid into the creek. They fished the boy out before he cashed in, but it was a close squeak. They couldn't blame the dog, of course not. Nothing else happened until late that fall.

"Brother Van Vranken was going to hold services in the Rock Creek schoolhouse and everybody turned out. There was a lot of snow for that time of the year, and Cal and his wife and little Sam piled into a sled and drove down. They shut

Bugler in the barn, but when they got to the schoolhouse, the dog had caught up with them, so Cal got a piece of string and tied him to the sled. The schoolhouse was full, and the stove was very enthusiastic. Brother Van announced he would open the meeting with prayer. Now this old duck that preached tonight didn't seem to be worried any about his religion, he seemed kind of comfortable and satisfied, but Brother Van's religion had set in on him and he took it awful serious.

"He got down on his knees and shut his eyes. He didn't do anything by halves, and the rest of us ducked our heads and looked at the warts on our fingers and tried to take in the prayer. Just then old Bugler trotted in the door and stood there wagging his tail for a minute. Then he walked over to Brother Van and looked him over and then he walked up a little closer and swiped that great long tongue of his right up one side of Van's face. He couldn't have done it at a worse time. Brother Van was saying, 'We beseech Thee, O Lord,' and I never heard so much emphasis on the 'O Lord,' in all my life, and that fool dog wouldn't quit. Of course none of us were supposed to be in on the game, but everyone could see what was going on, and finally Cal got up and tip-toed over to where he could get hold of the dog's collar. He always wore moccasins when he could and he didn't make any more noise than a cat, and just when he got hold of the dog's collar, Van fetched a vicious kick which landed on Cal's shin. Of course Cal didn't say anything, but I was peeking through my fingers and I saw him turn red as he dragged that dog out of the door in a hurry. Then he didn't come back, and by and by we heard a whistle. Now Cal wasn't musical, but he could whistle one tune, or part of it, and everybody in the country knew it. It was part of 'Pop, Goes the Weasel,' and after a while Mrs. Stevens got up kind of red in the face and went out and just as they were going out of the door, little Sam asked, 'Did man hurt papa?' Of course the rest of us stayed for a decision, but the sermon was pretty nearly a total wreck.

"It was the next summer when the dog business came to a head and bust. Cal was a great fisherman. He used to fish upper Rock Creek from his place clear to the first snow bank. He knew every hole and almost every fish in the creek. There was one old whale of a trout in a big hole about half a mile above his place who couldn't be tempted, and that trout began to get on Cal's nerves. He began to take twisted views of things and when he got a chance to get hold of a stick of dynamite, he was just desperate enough to use it. He got a piece of fuse and a cap and he made a kind of infernal machine and soaped it all up so it wouldn't get wet and went after that trout. I suppose you know what this dynamite is? It is about ten times as strong as blasting powder and is horribly skittish. Cal hadn't had any experience with it and he was nervous to begin with, but when he got to the edge of the creek and could see that trout fairly sneering at him, he lighted the fuse and threw the infernal machine into the water.

"Old Bugler was standing around wagging his tail all the time and when he saw the thing go into the water he jumped in after it. Cal had already started to run, but when he saw what Bugler was up to, he stopped running and commenced to fly. After he had covered about a hundred yards, he turned his head enough to see that the dog was right after him and then he let out another notch and ran until he was fairly beat. He fell down and was too weak to get up, so he just closed his eyes and chewed a piece of greasewood that happened to be sticking in his mouth. After he had died three or four times, he opened his eyes, then he lifted his head, and there right in front of him was that worthless dog, wet and happy and proud, with both paws on the giant powder! It was two years before Cal told me just how he killed that dog."

CHAPTER XXXV

A BOUT WITH THE JUDGE

WITH some twelve to thirty Montana appetites to be satisfied, you may be sure that our hotel kitchen was a busy place. The autocrat of this domain was a Chinaman named Chung. He was a very capable hotel cook. He had lived for more than thirty years in the West, coming to California in the early '50's as a boy of fourteen. Mother saw her first Chinese cooks in '79 when she came to Montana, and they met with her disapprobation. For years she maintained her hostile attitude until the summer of 1883, getting what help she could from transient female help and losing one capable cook after another by the matrimonial route.

We were planning a grand celebration and dance for July Fourth, and mother, who happened at that time to be struggling under multiplied burdens, gave her reluctant consent to my father's proposal that Chung, who was temporarily becalmed at Ubet by certain losses at poker, should be installed in the kitchen during the emergency. He did his work so well and so easily and so completely satisfied my mother's ideals of cleanliness, that after two weeks' probation, he was fairly adopted as a member of the family. He was, like most Chinamen, an inveterate gambler, but he withstood his successes and failures at the card table with commendable equanimity.

There was a great deal of work in handling the mail and the stage business, and the pay was small, but the stages brought our customers and thus we were indirectly compensated. The saloon business on the other hand was highly profitable even under our restrictions. Drinks and cigars were at the old level of two bits. Our beer was a celebrated Milwaukee brew, which came to us in bottles and cost fifty cents a quart. This was served in small glasses, five to the quart. Our cigars cost us eight cents apiece, giving us a higher percentage of profit. As I have said, the saloon was our club and was conducted in an orderly manner quite different from the rule generally prevailing. I can recall only three or four sporadic bouts at fisticuffs in my Ubet experience. I remember one occasion when two travelers, quarreling with each other when they arrived, seemed ready to lock horns and settle their differences in our midst. My father halted their warlike preparations and told them very gravely that we did not permit fighting, but if they really wanted to have it out, they could go down the Lewistown road about a quarter of a mile, where they would be on government land. "And," he added, "I hope you beat each other to death." Away they went in the moonlight, returning half an hour later somewhat damaged as to exterior, but otherwise much improved.

Occasionally some wayfarer, after a very moderate dosage of ardent spirits would develop pugilistic yearnings. To these I would propose a friendly bout with the gloves. I had been doing a good deal of boxing with some very skillful men and was quite competent in a defensive way, and as I was six feet tall and weighed one hundred and seventy pounds, I never had any difficulty in reducing pugilistic aspirations in my customers.

One of my most embarrassing encounters was when Fergus County was newly created, and Judge Bach was visiting the new county seat to open its first term of court. The Judge and his party, reaching Ubet by private conveyances, were held up by an unseasonable snowstorm. After breakfast, the party, which included stenographers, clients, and attorneys, came to the saloon, with a dull day in prospect, while they waited for fair weather. Then Judge Bach saw the boxing gloves hanging on the wall and they evoked immediate inquiry. He was told that I was the only one about the place who used them, and immediately I was urged to put them on. The idea of boxing with a Judge was something I could hardly consider. It will not do to say that the idea was abhorrent to me, it was rather incongruous or scandalous, but at last under his importunities, I consented, and we faced each other. The Judge was a young man about my height, but less muscular. He had undoubtedly done considerable sparring under instruction while in college and was fast and snappy. I contented myself with blocking and ducking and allowed the Judge to do all the work, and as he would occasionally get past my guard, he was having a very enjoyable time. This continued until he succeeded in landing a rather effective punch which made me forget all inhibitions, and I batted him soundly on the nose. This ended the bout, for the Judge bled freely and devoted himself to cold water and the sink for about twenty minutes, while I felt as I imagine a man would feel who had been found guilty of high treason.

Chapter XXXVI

CHEERY WEATHER

I RETAIN a very vivid impression of the sudden change of conditions during my early years in Montana. In the Musselshell in 1880, our life was unbelievably primitive. The three-acre field of oats was "cradled" and later in the fall was threshed by a method as old as the Scriptures. We drove a band of range horses into a round corral and kept them trotting round and round until they had trodden out the grain. It is safe to say that there was not a mile of fence in the whole valley. Poultry and eggs were scarce because eggs were not produced. We managed to have fresh milk, notwithstanding the likelihood that our milch cows would drift away with range cattle. What butter we used was brought in from older communities to the westward, packed in tins, and was an expensive luxury. Dirt floors were the rule in our cabins, although there was a board floor in our kitchen-dining room, and a puncheon floor in Gaugler's new store. All travelers in those days carried their necessary bedding and rolled their blankets under the stars, if the weather permitted, or sought whatever shelter offered in the inclement weather. There was one redeeming feature in our situation, in that we were *all* equally poor. The cattlemen and the prosperous wool grower lived in mud-daubed log hovels and were as ragged as the rest of us.

In six or seven years the situation was quite different. The roads were full of stage coaches, spring wagons, and buggies, and freight teams bringing our freight from the railroad in four or five days, and we could obtain almost everything found in the large markets. Barbed wire fences enclosed hay and grain fields, as well as the garden patches, and in the autumn we could hear the whirr of the thresher, and at last we had a plentiful supply of poultry, eggs, and fresh pork. Every little settlement had its school. We became conscious of politics and religion, as well as cultural matters. Game was becoming scarcer, although elk, deer, and antelope meat was common on our Ubet table, and we had excellent beef from our own herd. We bought three-year-old Cotswold wethers for three dollars apiece. You may be sure we still retained our character as meat eaters, although we had a large and productive garden.

My only justification in referring to early day weather is that, although the climate has not changed, we were more conscious of the stark, ruthless character of our sub-arctic winters. The traveler from Billings to Ubet might see in the course of the hundred-mile journey, seven or eight human habitations. He followed no graded turnpike, enclosed and delimited by fences, and should he in a storm stray a few feet from the track, he might never find it again.

I remember one morning after a smothering snow storm the village awoke to the fact that the Fort Benton stage had not arrived and almost immediately discovered that the missing conveyance, with its four horses tied to its wheels, was fifty feet off the road and not three hundred feet from the hotel. Under investigation we found the driver and three passengers sound asleep and comfortable within the closely curtained vehicle and were told that they lost the road in the blinding storm, and, although they knew they were near their destination, they had no stomach for blind wanderings. Stage drivers were the only people who were supposed to be on the road regardless of weather. During our occasional blizzards, often lasting for three days, everyone else prudently kept within shelter or close to it.

It is not necessary to tell the initiated that Montana weather is freakish. One autumn Paul McCormick made a hurried stage trip from Billings, and as the weather was very hot and the roads were dusty, he wore a broadbrimmed straw hat and a linen duster. When he was ready to return the next day, the weather had turned suddenly cold. There was a biting north wind, and frost was in the air. We loaned him a buffalo overcoat and he tied a silk handkerchief over his ears and went away, his costume completed most incongruously by the straw hat.

On another fall day, perhaps it was October, we had as guest a traveling salesman from an eastern firm. The autumn had been very warm, and our beds had not been supplied with the regular winter quota of blankets and comforters. In the middle of the night our eastern friend awoke with a suspicion which developed into a certainty that his room was getting cold. A young blizzard was sweeping in on a thirty-mile gale, and the thermometer had dropped about thirty degrees. He piled his clothing on the bed and lay there, sleeping little and shivering much, until he heard sounds of life below, when in much discomfort he clothed himself and came downstairs into the room between the dining room and parlor, which we referred to half humorously as the office. He found a radiant stove humming with newly supplied fuel, and in front of the stove the driver of the Billings stage, who had been facing the blizzard for seven hours. He had removed his heavy wraps and was standing by the stove endeavoring to thaw out the icicles which had frozen his mustache to his chin whiskers, for he was hungry, and until the ice barrier was removed he could have no satisfactory contact with breakfast. The salesman took one look at the ice-bound stage driver and exclaimed, "My God! what room did you have?" Within this year I heard that story over my radio, so I know it is long lived.

Chapter XXXVII

MONTANA CULTURE

O UR BODIES were well nourished and we always had a bountiful supply of good substantial food; we were kept comfortable in a variable sub-arctic climate by clothing which was serviceable without being modish, and there was warmth and comfort in the squat, unlovely, mud-topped log cabins. In the domain of culture, however, we were not so fortunate, our minds were occupied with the duties of the day. We feasted our eyes upon a vast and varied landscape, enlivened by the presence of wild game and saved from monotony by shifting cloud shadows. Our ears were delighted and stirred by the music of Nature with her entire gamut of sounds, from the shrilling of insects to the *fortissimo* crash of thunder reverberating from mountain cliffs. We were witnessing and taking our parts in that great drama, "The Subjugation of the Wilderness," without appreciating the fact. Of music in the accepted sense we had none. Ubet in the old days boasted no instrument more pretentious than the harmonica. The fiddlers who played for our dances were imported from distant settlements.

In matters artistic we were hopeless. Our dining room was not in bad taste, but our parlor was criminal. Besides a few inoffensive family photographs we had on its walls a panel which had once been the top of a cigar box, painted by myself. My subject was a yellow rose and it was handled with geometric precision, the result being a flower such as might have been created by a careful artisan in sheet brass. Then there was the basswood scoop shovel decorated with a snow scene, but the unkindest cut of all was that chromo which, in its massy gilt frame, had followed the family from Wisconsin. It was a major offense about sixteen inches by twenty, and it was called "The Easter Cross." The artisan who had produced the original had depicted a rocky islet surrounded by a tumultuous green sea. The sky, also green, could be distinguished from the sea by the absence of waves. Surmounting the sedimentary sandstone of the rocky isle, was a squat masonry cross and about it there was entwined a passion flower in full bloom. This pictorial treasure places us in the stone age of art, beyond question.

We devoted one winter to studying and rehearsing a melodrama entitled "The Last Loaf." Almost the entire population was in the cast. Ben

Stevens had a comedy part and he practiced stuttering so assiduously that it took him three years to break himself of the habit. The drama was never produced, because we had an early spring and the call to work could not be ignored.

In spite of our cultural deprivations, we were intellectually alert. There was in the West a very small proportion of numbskulls. We read good magazines and good books. We had two daily newspapers, received within three or four days of their publication, and our reading was discussed and digested. We were interested in science and in politics and could discuss intelligently the questions that were treated superficially by men of national reputation.

We wasted much of our time, of course, playing cards or billiards or in the manufacture of fancy horse equipment, such as quirts, bridles, and *jaquimas*, and frittered away many golden hours in the telling of stories. Every man had at least one story which had stood the test of time and like Jefferson's "Rip Van Winkle" could be relied upon to hold its audience.

CHAPTER XXXVIII

THE CIRCULAR STORY

ONE WINTER night a chinook was blowing and the soft snow was filling the air to the height of twenty feet. The building was trembling and creaking under the varying stresses, and the entire male population was gathered in the saloon. A quiet game of draw poker was in progress but was not so exciting that the players could not listen to the story which a visiting sheepherder had to tell. We had been discussing the old stories about creasing wild horses. Then we had various stories of the pursuit of wild horses by men afoot. The question was academic, for at that time, horses were cheap and wild horses almost nonexistent.

Our sheep herder obtained the floor: "Well, gentlemen, four years ago I was working for Ralph Berry on the Musselshell, and there was a 'shavetail' come along buying wethers. Berry had about six hundred that this feller wanted, but he didn't want 'em if he couldn't throw 'em in with another bunch he had bought over by Black Butte, so they wanted me to take a letter down to Flat Willow and meet the Black Butte outfit, so that the two bunches could be throwed together at the Mussel-shell crossing, but they didn't tell me all of this, but just gave me a horse and told me to deliver the letter.

"Well, gentlemen, I started out early in the morning and was getting along all right until I was about ten miles beyond the Lavina road. And then wha' d' you know? The letter was gone! Well, gentlemen, it was a still day so the letter wouldn't blow around, so I took the back trail. I had to go slow, of course, but finally I found it, but I lost a lot of time, so I had to sleep out that night. Just after sundown I stopped at a little creek where there was some big cottonwoods, so I unsaddled and watered my horse and picketed him to a sagebrush and then sat down to eat the lunch Mrs. Berry had give me. While I was a setting and eating my sandwiches, I looked up in the tree and I saw a dead Injun. He was up there on a big limb, all wrapped up in his buffalo robes and tied on good and plenty, and about the time I got through eating I began to wonder if I couldn't get him down somehow. Some people think that's just like robbing a grave, but it doesn't seem so to me; he couldn't stay up there forever. Some day he'd fall off his perch, and I can't see what difference it makes whether it's sooner or later. The scientific ducks are digging 'em up all the time in Egypt, and nobody makes a fuss, so I got hold of a branch that hung down and took a run at it and then let go and sure enough the old boy flopped off and turned over two or three times and hit the ground.

"Well, gentlemen, I was kind of sorry I'd done it. There he was, the old robes busted open clear up to his neck. They was thin and brittle like paper, and of course nobody could ever get him back again. There wasn't much left of him except bones. He had about ten feet of heavy brass wire wrapped around each wrist for bracelets, and there was a dipper made from the horn of a mountain sheep, and a spoon of buffalo horn, and a thing-um-a-jig that they carry live coals in, and some red and yellow paint, just what they generally put in so a feller can start housekeeping.

"Then I found a little bundle, and when I opened it up wha' d' you know? It was a Bible! That floored me. I couldn't see what in hell a Bible was doing in a place like that. When I tried to open it up it kinda stuck together and then crumbled so there wasn't a chance of saving it, but when the cover come off I saw some writing and wha' d' you know? It was, 'To Willy, with Mother's love.' That made me feel kind of funny, for my name is Bill and mother always called me Willy.

"Well, gentlemen, I took a stick and opened up

his upper end and I never got such a start in my life. His hair was yellow and curly and he had whiskers! He was a squaw man, sure enough, and that explained the Bible. And gentlemen, wha' d' you know, as soon as I found he was a white man I wanted to bury him, but of course there was no chance. And when I lay down on my saddle blanket I couldn't go to sleep. I just lay there thinking about that feller and how he had turned Injun and had held onto his Bible. And I tried to imagine his funeral when he cashed in and his squaw had packed the Bible in with him for his 'medicine.'

"Along about midnight my horse whinnied and I started straight up. You know how a horse whinnies when you come back from a trip and turn him out in his home pasture, and we were out and all alone, twenty miles from anybody, and then he took a run, broke loose, and away he went.

"I had plenty of time between then and day-break to make up my mind what to do, and I just said to myself, 'I'm no quitter, I'll walk that horse down if I put in the rest of my life. I'm going to camp on his trail.' And as soon as it was daylight I took my rifle and started out. The trail followed the east side of the creek; we were going north up towards the Snowies. After about three miles the trail turned sharp to the right over some high hills where the grass was dry, but I had no trouble in following it, because he was dragging his rope.

"Every time I would raise a ridge, I expected to see him, for the signs were fresh, but there was nothing in sight, not even game. Everything I saw was out of range and I was getting hungry. We must have covered fifteen miles or so on an easterly course, and I was about ready to leave the trail to do some hunting when I shot a jack rabbit. He was tough and stringy, but them was the qualities I had to have in my business. And when I got through with him, there wasn't enough left to bait a trap.

"Come dusk, I lay down under some willows in a little draw and went bang to sleep as soon as I hit the ground. I was dead tired. But some time in the middle of the night, I heard that horse whinny again, and right close to, and it worried me. But I got to sleep again and the sun was shining when I waked up. The trail was leading south now, towards the Musselshell, and followed down a little creek. I thought I ought to get a shot at a white-tail, for I was nearly starved, but no such luck. Then we left the creek when we was within three miles of the river and started west over some awfully rough country. After about ten or twelve miles of that kind of work I was about played out, but I gritted my teeth and said, 'I'm no quitter.' I didn't see how that horse was going to last forever, and after a while I killed an old sage-hen.

And when I had cooked and eaten her, all except the feet, I felt she had the same qualities as the jack rabbit.

"Late in the afternoon the trail turned northerly along the creek, and I followed it until dark, stopping to rest once in a while, for I was getting leg weary. And I just fell down and went to sleep. I was sure camping on the trail. About midnight I waked up to hear that horse whinny again, and as soon as it was daylight I took my rifle and started out."

At this point a growing suspicion had taken definite form in my mind. Could it be possible that the guileless shepherd was trying to put over a circular story? I glanced at Billy Coates. He responded by lifting a significant eyebrow. The narrator was continuing—

"Every time I would raise a ridge, I expected to see him, for the signs were fresh, but there was nothing in sight, not even game. Everything I saw was out of range and I was getting hungry. We must have covered fifteen miles or so on an easterly course and I was about ready to leave the trail to do some hunting when I shot a jack rabbit. He was tough and stringy, but them was the qualities I had to have in my business. And when I got through with him there wasn't enough left to bait a trap.

"Come dusk, I lay down under some willows in a little draw and went bang to sleep as soon as I hit the ground. I was dead tired. But some time in the middle of the night, I heard a horse whinny again, and right close to, and it worried me. But I got to sleep again and the sun was shining when I waked up. The trail was leading south now, towards the Musselshell."

My suspicions were entirely confirmed. I looked around to see an interchange of knowing glances and winks. We were all wise except a silent man who was sitting near the cue rack; he had come in after supper on the belated Benton coach. He manifested a growing interest in the story, for the sheepherder's attention was concentrated upon him as the only possible victim of his hoax.

"Then we left the creek when we was within three miles of the river and started west over some awfully rough country. After about ten or twelve miles of that kind of work, I was about played out, but I gritted my teeth and said, 'I'm no quitter.' I didn't see how that horse was going to last forever, and after a while I killed an old sage-hen. And when I had cooked and eaten her, all except the feet, I felt she had the same qualities as the jack rabbit.

"Late in the afternoon the trail turned northerly ..."And on and on around and around the circle the story continued. At last the silent man brought out from an inside pocket a paper tablet and lead pencil and interrupted the story by saying in a harsh monotone, "I am deaf, will you please write it?"

The story teller turned a despairing eye towards those of us who had escaped his snare and said, with a gesture of frustration, "Oh, what's the use!"

* * *

Perhaps I am touched by the contagion of despair. I have tried to tell you some of the happenings in my long life, but after all this effort I find I have completed only one-tenth of my task. Then when I remember that in all the centuries that have passed since Moses took his pen in hand and described his own funeral there has been no completed autobiography, the thought is so discouraging that I bring my story to a close and say, "Goodbye."